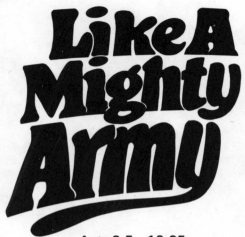

Like A Mighty Army

Acts 8:5—12:25

by Abe C. Van Der Puy
Voice of Missions
Back to the Bible

D1359002

Back to the Bible

Lincoln, Nebraska 68501

42,000 printed to date—1987
(5-5268—42M—77)
ISBN 0-8474-0715-2

Printed in the United States of America

Dedication

To Betty and Stan Harwood,
partners with us for many years
through prayer and material support
toward helping to complete the greatest
of all enterprises—world evangelization.

"Now he who plants and he who waters are one,
and each one will receive his own reward
according to his own labor" (I Cor. 3:8).

Introduction

The title for this book comes from the hymn "Onward, Christian Soldiers." The first part of one stanza of that hymn declares, "Like a Mighty Army moves the Church of God." The Book of Acts presents the thrilling picture of the Church marching forward in Jesus' name and in the power of the Holy Spirit. Another stanza of that hymn reminds us of Christ's promise: "I will build my church; and the gates of hell shall not prevail against it" (Matt. 16:18, KJV).

> Crowns and thrones may perish, kingdoms rise and wane,
> But the Church of Jesus constant will remain,
> Gates of hell can never 'gainst that Church prevail;
> We have Christ's own promise, and that cannot fail.

In the first volume, I suggested the following outline for the Book of Acts:

  I. The Church Enlisted (1:1—8:4)
 II. The Church Equipped (8:5—12:25)
III. The Church Commissioned (13:1—20:38)
IV. The Church Reinforced (21:1—28:31)

In this book we'll look at the Church's being equipped by God for larger service. The apostles, church leaders and new believers needed the

5

patient teaching of the Holy Spirit as He prepared them for the great task of preaching the Gospel to everyone everywhere as Christ had commissioned them to do. The Church continued to experience its baptism of fire as determined enemies tried everything possible to harass and even eliminate the followers of Christ. But they did not succeed in their wicked plans. In fact, with great dismay, they witnessed the conversion to Christ of their most zealous cohort, Saul of Tarsus. His story alone would make this part of Acts of utmost importance. Thank God for His awesome power, which can change Saul the persecutor into Paul the missionary of Christ!

I believe we will find great help and instruction for our own lives if we seek to identify with the people and experiences we find in this section of Acts. The same Holy Spirit who faithfully prepared those early believers can prepare us, too, for effective outreach. They faced immense changes and challenges, just as we do. This could cause us to be fearful, but the message of Acts is that the Holy Spirit can equip us to meet those changes and challenges.

Today, as followers of Christ and members of His Church, we face an overwhelming responsibility. More than half of the world's population has not yet heard the message of salvation. We have Christ's command to take the Good News to them. Every believer who has been equipped and trained by the Holy Spirit and who trusts in His limitless power can obey Jesus' commission. Therefore, let's march forward to join Philip and Peter and Paul as they received the Spirit's teaching for service. Let's travel with those early church members as they learned the lessons designed by God to equip them for ministry in the Spirit. Let's watch as God shattered their prejudices and enlarged their vision. We'll discover that the Holy Spirit's power and principles haven't changed. If we walk in obedience and submission to the Lord, we'll have the joy of serving our generation as those Spirit-filled believers did theirs.

Let's adopt the prayer of Bessie P. Head as she expressed it in her hymn "O Breath of Life":

> O Breath of Life, come sweeping through us,
> Revive Your Church with life and power;
> O Breath of Life, come, cleanse, renew us,
> And fit Your Church to meet this hour.
>
> Revive us, Lord! Is zeal abating
> While harvest fields are vast and white?
> Revive us, Lord—the world is waiting!
> Equip Your Church to spread the light.

Contents

Chapter 1

And in Samaria
(Acts 8:5-25)

The Book of Acts describes the enlistment and equipping of the Church for service. In it we find a modern-day pattern for evangelism and fellowship. With the enabling power of the Holy Spirit, the early church grew from a small band of 120 followers in the upper room to a vigorous army of more than 5000 within a short time. Even persecution and imprisonment did not dampen the believers' desire to preach the Gospel.

But then the early church suffered its first martyrdom as Stephen was stoned by the Jewish officials. The opening verses of Acts 8 paint an apparently bleak picture for the Church. They focus on three serious facts. *First*, "devout men carried Stephen to his burial, and made great lamentation over him" (v. 2). The believers had lost a great leader, and they were experiencing genuine sorrow. In their grief it would have been easy for them to lose their faith. *Second*, the followers of Christ "were all scattered throughout the regions of Judea

9

and Samaria, except the apostles" (v. 1). It looked momentarily as though the Church had been dealt a fatal blow from which it would not recover. *Third*, we read: "As for Saul, he made havoc of the church" (v. 3). Under the leadership of Saul, the persecution intensified. It appeared for a time that he was going to win in his efforts to wipe out Christianity.

However, as we will see, this persecution was part of the Lord's plan and eventually led to even greater progress and growth. Before ascending into heaven, Jesus had promised His followers that they would witness in Jerusalem, Judea, Samaria and the ends of the earth (see 1:8). Until that time, however, the believers had limited their witness to Jerusalem. This persecution was needed to get the believers moving. But even more important was the way in which they responded to the persecution: "Therefore those who were scattered went everywhere preaching the word" (8:4). Instead of hiding or renouncing their faith in Christ, they continued to witness boldly. They did not allow the threat of death to deter them from fulfilling the Lord's Great Commission.

Time and time again in the history of Christianity, we have seen this same phenomenon occurring. Instead of destroying the Church, persecution serves to spur it on to greater dedication and growth. As W. Graham Scroggie has stated, "The devil's breath has fanned the flames of the gospel. The bruised tree has filled the air with perfume" (*The Acts of the Apostles,* p. 66).

10

Christians are the strongest when they are bruised and bleeding. This was true of the early church, and it is still true today. A number of years ago, the Christians in Colombia, South America, suffered ten years of intense persecution. What happened? The number of believers increased dramatically during that time. The church became stronger, and the believers grew spiritually.

The church in China presents a similar picture. During the rule of Chairman Mao, believers in that country were oppressed terribly. We all wondered what was taking place behind the Bamboo Curtain. Now we know. The church not only survived, but it grew dramatically. I have had the privilege of visiting China on two occasions recently and can testify to the dynamic vitality of that persecuted church. The example of these churches—and of the early church—shows us that the Holy Spirit can, and will, guide and strengthen us in even the most difficult circumstances.

Color-blind Philip

With this in mind, let's look at some specifics of the Church's advance. The spotlight focuses first on Philip. Who was this man? We first met him in Acts 6, where the Jerusalem church chose him to be one of the seven deacons. We see him again in Acts 21. There we learn that he had settled in Caesarea and that he had four virgin daughters who prophesied (see vv. 8,9). But, of course, Philip is best known as an evangelist. Even though he was

11

no doubt doing important work as a deacon, the Lord chose to add a whole new dimension to his ministry, giving him an effective evangelistic gift.

The Lord still works in this manner today. Frequently He takes the most unlikely people and places them in an area of service they never expected. He often calls us to serve Him in ways we never dreamed possible. And when He calls us for a particular task, we can be assured that He will equip us to perform it. Therefore, we should always be ready for God's call, waiting to respond immediately to His command.

When the Lord called Philip to be an evangelist, note how he responded: "Then Philip went down to the city of Samaria and preached Christ to them" (8:5). Even though he was facing severe persecution and may have had fears about witnessing, Philip obeyed his Saviour implicitly. Philip's actions are even more remarkable in light of the social atmosphere of that day. The Jews refused to associate with the Samaritans, who were considered to be half-breeds. Up until that time, this same attitude was still prevalent in the early church. The Christians had been preaching only to the Jews.

The Jews' hatred of the Samaritans went back to the time of the Israelites' captivity in Assyria. When the Assyrians captured Samaria in 722 B.C., they transported some of the Jews back to Assyria. They then brought other peoples into Samaria. Consequently, the Jews that were left in Samaria intermarried with the new immigrants. The resulting race eventually established their own ritual and built their own temple on Mt. Gerizim.

The mixed ancestry and differences in worship of the Samaritans aggravated the purist Jews. The Lord Jesus constantly battled this prevailing attitude toward the Samaritans. The incident described in Luke 9:51-56 is a prime example. Jesus wanted to enter a village of the Samaritans but was refused. Then James and John said, "Lord, do You want us to command fire to come down from heaven and consume them, just as Elijah did?" (v. 54). The Lord rebuked them for this attitude. He showed the disciples what their attitude should be as He frequently associated with the Samaritans. He lovingly gave the message of life to the Samaritan woman by the well (see John 4:5-26). When Jesus wanted to illustrate who is a good neighbor, He told the story of the *good* Samaritan (see Luke 10:30-37).

Philip overcame the racism and prejudices of his day and followed the Lord's example in boldly proclaiming the Good News to the Samaritans. Every believer who is sincerely following Jesus should do the same. I have seen this happening in many parts of the world today. Recently my wife and I spent some time ministering on Operation Mobilisation's ship, the *M. V. Logos*. We were impressed when we saw how the crew members from 28 different nations served together with mutual respect for each other in Christ. That's the way it should be. Christianity is color blind. It makes no distinctions. Colossians 3:11 emphatically states, "There is neither Greek nor Jew, circumcised nor uncircumcised, barbarian, Scythian, slave nor free, but Christ is all and in all."

Joyful Samaritans

When we are obeying the will of our Lord, our labors will not go unrewarded. Philip's preaching in Samaria brought tremendous results. Acts 8:8 says simply but eloquently, "And there was great joy in that city." We are told, "The multitudes with one accord heeded the things spoken by Philip" (v. 6). Why did these Samaritans respond to Philip's preaching? They recognized the truth of the Gospel message, and they saw the miracles performed by Philip. The Samaritans realized that God's power was present, and they readily responded to the message, to the healings and to the casting out of evil spirits (see vv. 6,7).

It's great to know that God still works powerfully today. Lately I have seen and heard about many miraculous transformations that have taken place in the lives of people who have accepted Jesus Christ as their Saviour. One woman was suffering the effects of having been abused as a child. Then, not long ago, she had a personal encounter with Jesus Christ. Her life now has new hope and joy. Furthermore, she has led 230 other people to Christ in just eight months. While this may seem impossible, it is true. The Lord Jesus has been working through this woman. Consequently, the great joy in her life has overflowed into her community, just as it did from Philip's life to the people of Samaria.

This always happens when the Lord Jesus takes full control. When we respond to the Lord's message, we have joy in our personal lives, in our homes, in our cities and in our countries. Some time ago, my wife and I met a couple whom the Lord had saved. At one time they seemed to have everything going for them. But God was not in their thoughts. They fell into the trap of alcoholism, drugs and immorality. Their lives went from bad to worse. Then, through a series of circumstances, they began to consider the claims of the Lord Jesus on their lives. Judy and Richard believed in Him as Saviour and acknowledged Him as Lord. Jesus Christ made their lives new. Now they have a beautiful testimony and overflowing joy. God is using them to lead others to Christ, who in turn are experiencing joy that is full.

Power-Hungry Simon

Among this joyful group of Samaritans who heard and responded to Philip's message was a man named Simon. He was a sorcerer who claimed to have magical power. It's possible that he was in league with evil spirits. For a long time he had been impressing the people of Samaria with his magic. They believed that he had great power from God and listened to him (see Acts 8:9-11). However, when Philip worked genuine miracles in the Lord's power, Simon's magical power seemed small indeed. Philip's words and miracles may have caused Simon to realize what a fake he really was. Whatever Simon's motives were, the Bible tells us that he "also believed; and when he was baptized he continued with Philip" (v. 13).

However, Simon's old desire for power soon got the best of him. When the church at Jerusalem heard of the conversions in Samaria, they sent Peter and John there. As the apostles prayed for the Samaritan believers and laid hands on them, they received the Holy Spirit. When Simon saw this, he tried to buy the power to bestow the gift of the Holy Spirit (see vv. 14-19). The act of trying to buy ecclesiastical power is known today as simony.

Notice Peter's stern answer to Simon: "Your money perish with you, because you thought that the gift of God could be purchased with money! You have neither part nor portion in this matter, for your heart is not right in the sight of God" (vv. 20,21). Why was Peter so stern? Because he needed to teach Simon—and us—that money can never purchase spiritual blessings or power. We must meet certain moral qualifications—principally faith in the Lord Jesus and dedication to His teachings. Instead of wanting to buy the power to bestow the Holy Spirit, Simon should simply have desired the power of the Holy Spirit in his own life.

Although we may not be as crass as Simon, we can also make the mistake of thinking that material wealth or outward ceremony can buy favor with God. We may be tempted to think like the people of Jesus' day, who said to Him, "What shall we do, that we may work the works of God?" (John 6:28). Christ's answer to them is still the only answer He gives to us: "This is the work of God, that you believe in Him whom He sent" (v. 29). This is one reason why the Reformation was so important—it reemphasized the glorious truth that true blessings come not by our merits or possessions or mere outward rituals but by simple trust in the Lord. The hymnwriter expressed it beautifully when he wrote: "My hope is built on nothing less / Than Jesus' blood and righteousness."

It's important to remember this truth. We must constantly remind ourselves that we are saved by God's grace alone, not by our wealth or our works. In this regard, we should heed the words of G. Campbell Morgan, who said, "If the Church believed that today, and acted upon it, she might lack a good deal she possesses, but would be richer for the lack. There is a lack that means power; there is a possession that means paralysis" (*The Acts of the Apostles*, p. 209).

Many people have asked, "Was Simon a Christian?" While we can venture a guess, only God knows for sure. He alone can judge Simon's motives. Although the Bible indicates that Simon believed and was baptized, he didn't seem to understand basic spiritual principles. Even his last prayer seemed more concerned about the danger of punishment than the fact that he had sinned (see Acts 8:24). Let the case of Simon be a warning to us. We cannot buy God's favors and His power with money, good works or an outward show of piety. The Bible clearly states, "God is Spirit, and those who worship Him must worship in spirit and truth" (John 4:24). "The Father is seeking such to worship Him"

17

(v. 23). The Samaritans understood this important truth and expressed a genuine faith in Christ. As a result, they became the recipients of God's wonderful blessings.

Cooperative Apostles

As we have seen, when the church at Jerusalem heard what was happening in Samaria, the leaders sent Peter and John to observe and to help. It's encouraging to see that Peter and John were working well together. They had very different personalities and temperaments. By nature, they could have clashed constantly. However, the Lord had tied them together in a great purpose. They emphasized their oneness in Christ instead of their differences. So together and united they came to Samaria.

From their reaction to the evangelization of Samaria, it also becomes apparent that their attitude toward the Samaritans had changed. Notice that Peter and John didn't criticize Philip for preaching the Gospel to the Samaritans. This is significant when we consider the fact that John was one of the men who had wanted to call down fire on the Samaritans (see Luke 9:54). They were finally beginning to understand that the Gospel was for everyone. Certainly Peter still needed to learn more on that subject. (Don't we all?) And Jesus would teach it to him dramatically in his experience with Cornelius (see Acts 10). But even now Peter and John were in total agreement with what Philip had done. They shared in the joy of the evangelist, the people and the whole city. In fact, the Bible tells us that Peter and John laid hands on the new believers so that they would receive the Holy Spirit (see 8:15-17).

This whole episode raises an important question: *Don't believers ordinarily receive the Holy Spirit at the time of conversion and faith?* The answer is an emphatic *yes.* To the believers at Pentecost Peter said, "Repent, and let every one of you be baptized in the name of Jesus Christ for the remission of sins; and you shall receive the gift of the Holy Spirit" (Acts 2:38). Ephesians 1:13 also states, "In Him you also trusted, after you heard the word of truth, the gospel of your salvation; in whom also, having believed, you were sealed with the Holy Spirit of promise."

If this is true, how then can we explain the delay in the case of the Samaritans? Why was it necessary for Peter and John to lay hands on them in order to bestow the gift of the Holy Spirit? I think we can find a simple explanation: What Peter and John did constituted another but smaller Pentecost. It was God's way of showing the apostles and other Jewish Christians that the Samaritans were no less important than the Jews. We see this same outpouring of the Holy Spirit in the conversion of Cornelius (a Gentile) and his household in Acts 10. These experiences underscore the fact that Jesus died for Jews, Samaritans and Gentiles. His blessings, including the great blessing of the Holy Spirit, belong to all believers, regardless of race, background or condition!

The footnote to this story presents a beautiful picture of Peter's and John's change in attitude.

Acts 8:25 states, "So when they had testified and preached the word of the Lord, they returned to Jerusalem, preaching the gospel in many villages of the Samaritans." We see by their actions that they not only approved of Philip's ministry but they also entered enthusiastically into it themselves. It must have been quite a sight to watch these genuine Jews evangelizing among the Samaritans. It's very possible that some of these Samaritans recognized them as Jesus' companions and knew of the apostles' negative attitudes toward them in the past. No doubt they were surprised by the change that had taken place in Peter and John. They saw how the overflowing love of the Lord Jesus had made a difference in their lives. Peter and John had experienced the transforming power of salvation. They had no intention of keeping the Gospel for a select few. They wanted to share that great message with everyone. And the Samaritans readily responded to such a message.

Since all the words of Scripture are significant, it is important to note that Peter and John did their evangelizing in "many" villages of the Samaritans. I'm sure they didn't take the most direct or easiest route back to Jerusalem. Their return could wait. They knew that they must minister in many places while the opportunity existed. They weren't satisfied just to exercise leadership in Jerusalem. They desired to be where the action was. May God help us to follow their example. Countless cities and areas of the world are still waiting for the Gospel. These people will hear only as burdened followers reach out to them with Christ's message of salvation.

In Acts 8 we learn some important lessons about evangelism. The witness of Philip teaches us, first of all, that Christianity is color blind. Like this evangelist, we need to break through the racial barriers and prejudices that exist in the world, and in many of our churches, in order to preach the Gospel to those who still need to hear. Second, the response of the Samaritans shows us the true joy that evangelism brings, not only to the hearer but to the speaker as well. Third, we see the power of the Gospel. As evangelists, we must be careful how we use the power given to us by the Holy Spirit. The example of Simon warns us of the danger of seeking power for power's sake. May we never depart from the simplicity that is in Christ. Finally, the attitude of the apostles teaches us the importance of cooperation and direct involvement in evangelism. They understood what God was doing and joined in enthusiastically. They weren't satisfied with being the "big guys" in Jerusalem. They vigorously engaged in grass-roots evangelism. Because of their attitude, the Church was being equipped for even larger impact and outreach. When we learn to follow their example, then we, too, will begin to see great things happen.

Chapter 2

Everywhere With the Gospel—
Even in a Desert
(Acts 8:26-40)

Many of you may remember the film *Through Gates of Splendor,* which tells the story of the martyrdom of five young men who were trying to reach the Auca Indians in Ecuador for Christ. At the end of the film, Elisabeth Elliot, wife of one of those slain, made an interesting statement. She declared, "They [the Aucas who killed the missionaries] had their reasons; God had His." When you first hear that statement, you're tempted to say, "Elisabeth, did I hear you correctly? Surely you must be mistaken." But Elisabeth Elliot was absolutely right. Although the death of those five dedicated missionaries seemed like a senseless waste at the time, the years since that tragedy have revealed God's perfect reasons for permitting this seeming disaster. The impact of the Auca story goes on and on. My wife and I have seen many people called into the Lord's service through the example of these men. We have also met many individuals who have trusted Christ as their Saviour after seeing the film or reading the story of their lives. Even the Aucas who killed these missionaries have come to know the Lord through the testimony and example of those who later entered the tribe to continue the work of the martyred men.

We learn a great lesson from this. God always has His reasons for everything that happens, even when we don't think so. We often wonder and complain about the circumstances God allows. But later we see His reasons for them. When I find that God has placed me in a difficult situation, I remember His great promise to me in Revelation 3:8: "See, I have set before you an open door, and no one can shut it; for you have a little strength, have kept My word, and have not denied My name." This promise assures us that when we trust God's strength, follow His Word and honor His name, then even strange circumstances will turn out to be an open door for service. The story before us in Acts 8 illustrates this truth in a wonderful way.

Strange Circumstances

Philip was engaged in a flourishing ministry in Samaria. He had laid the foundation for evangelism in this area, and many were coming to know the Lord. Then, at the height of his ministry there, he received a strange order from the Lord. God's angel told him to leave Samaria and travel on the Jerusalem-Gaza road to the desert. No doubt Philip was confused about God's reasons for giving such a command. This strategy didn't seem to make sense at all. Philip may have wondered if he was being punished in some way. Why else would God make

23

him abandon his ministry and send him into the desert?

Maybe you have faced a similar experience when it seemed as though God was taking you away from opportunities and consigning you to the desert. Abram must have felt this way when God told him to leave his homeland and head for an unknown country (see Gen. 12:1-3). Paul must have had some second thoughts when he tried to go into Bithynia and was prevented from doing so (see Acts 16:6,7). Of course, we know that God had a special purpose in mind for both of these men as He directed them. But what about the negative factors that seem to curtail our service? Maybe you are hindered by poor health. Or perhaps you are experiencing economic problems. Or you are facing work disappointments that appear to be terrible demotions. Or maybe you'd just like to see more obvious fruit in your service. Whatever your problems may be, no doubt they look like a vast desert to you. Take heart. God has His reasons. In His time He makes the desert blossom like a rose. He promises to provide an open door for service in every situation.

In this regard, we can be encouraged by the experiences of two great men of faith. Famed author Francis Schaeffer spent a great deal of time patiently serving in relative obscurity at the L'Abri center in the little Swiss town of Huémoz. During that time, God was preparing him and his wife for larger service. The foundation was being laid for a worldwide ministry through books, lectures and

24

films. What seemed like a desert became a land of opportunity for him.

Likewise, the conversion of Charles Haddon Spurgeon shows us the importance of every ministry, however small. One wintry night he entered a little church. There were only a few people in attendance at the service. The pastor was speaking on the text, "Look to Me, and be saved, all you ends of the earth!" (Isa. 45:22). As this pastor preached that night, he must have thought that God had sent him to a desert devoid of significant opportunity. But God used his ministry and message that night to reach Charles Haddon Spurgeon. That preacher soon realized that God had given him a marvelous door of opportunity.

Like these men, Philip may have found the Lord's directions confusing. Nevertheless, when he received God's order to "arise and go" (Acts 8:26), he immediately left his work and went into the desert (see v. 27). Even though he didn't understand God's purposes, he trusted God to lead him in the desert. Obedience is the key that unlocks God's door of opportunity and blessing.

Great Guidance

When Philip arrived in the desert, he discovered he was not alone. A man from Ethiopia was traveling on the same road. Once again Philip received a direct message from God, as the Spirit instructed him, "Go near and overtake this chariot" (Acts 8:28). Suddenly everything made sense to Philip. The Lord had led him to the desert for this purpose.

The Holy Spirit had given him precise guidance that had placed him in the right place at the right time. The desert didn't seem to be a lonely or limiting place any longer. It was a land of opportunity!

While the Lord was leading Philip to the place where He wanted him, He was also preparing the traveler and his retinue to receive the message. The Ethiopian eunuch was a man who longed to know God. He was returning from Jerusalem, where he had gone to worship. Furthermore, he was reading a key messianic passage in Isaiah 53 (see Acts 8:27,28). His heart was ready to receive the message that Philip would give him. God, in His perfect timing, had opened the way. Philip simply needed to obey.

Through all the twists and turns of life, God will do the same for us when we really seek to be His witnesses. He will arrange for prepared people to be met by the right witnesses. On many occasions I have seen the Lord turn disturbing and unusual circumstances in my life into great open doors of opportunity.

When we were missionaries with HCJB in Quito, Ecuador, we lived on the outskirts of the city about five miles north of the mission. Eucalyptus groves surrounded our house, which sat on a lot that was subdivided from a large hacienda, or ranch. The center of the ranch had been left intact, and a large group of Indians met there once a year for a big religious fiesta. It was never very long before this celebration turned into a drinking spree.

One Sunday, my wife and I were awakened in the

middle of the night by loud noises that sounded like gunfire. After the initial shock, we realized that the fiesta was in progress. The sounds we heard were caused by fireworks. We succeeded in dozing several hours more, until we were roused again just before dawn by loud band music. We peered through our bedroom windows and saw a large procession of people with lighted candles passing by on the narrow road. This time we couldn't go back to sleep. Instead, we had devotions together and prayed specifically that God would allow us to witness in some way to the people at the fiesta. Even as we made this strange request, we couldn't help wondering how the Lord could give us an open door among drunken people at a fiesta.

In the afternoon we took a walk in the direction of the hacienda center. As we did, three drunk men came wobbling up the road toward us. One man was carrying a large cassette recorder. He came right up to me, shoved the recorder toward my face and said, "Cante [sing]." When I didn't sing for him, he commanded, "Entonces, hable [speak then]." And speak I did for quite some time, as the machine recorded every word. I told him about our Gospel radio station. I recited Scripture verses on salvation. I clearly explained God's plan of salvation. Then, satisfied, he and his friends stumbled on their way. I've often wondered about the look on his face when he played the recording the next day. The Lord knew that I could not have witnessed to him in his drunken stupor, so He gave me the opportunity to share the Gospel via a recording that could be

27

played again and again when he was sober. I fully expect to meet that man again some day and am trusting that he's still listening to that message of life. God answered our prayer in a wonderful way, guiding us through this open door in strange circumstances. He will do the same for you when you willingly submit to His great guidance, just as Philip did.

Effective Witness

Philip followed the Spirit's guidance and approached the chariot of the Ethiopian (see Acts 8:30). Like us, he may have had some apprehensions about witnessing to this stranger. But he trusted the Lord to give him the words to speak. As he drew near, he heard the eunuch reading from Isaiah. Rather than approaching the man with a prepared speech or pat declarations, Philip instead started with a question of interest to the Ethiopian. He asked the man, "Do you understand what you are reading?" (v. 30). And he received a humble reply, "How can I, unless someone guides me?" (v. 31). The eunuch then invited Philip to join him in the chariot and explain the passage to him. Philip began with this man's need and, as a result, was given an opportunity to share the Gospel with him.

We can often witness effectively by asking questions. Too often we barge in and dominate the conversation with matters especially interesting to us. Ask questions that demonstrate your interest in the person whom you are seeking to reach for Christ. Often it isn't long until the individual opens up and expresses a need. Soon he will ask for help, and then you can freely share Christ with him. When our witness is bathed in prayer and guided by the Holy Spirit, we will then begin to see the way opening up for us.

We have some friends whom the Lord is using wonderfully to reach people with the Gospel. They frequently use the question method of witnessing. They invite a number of friends to their home for an evening meal. They always make sure to include an unsaved couple whom they have met through normal, everyday encounters. Then they make sure they spend time learning more about the guest couple. This often leads to further opportunities for contact, and eventually they find an open door for leading the people to Christ.

On our recent trips to China we found many opportunities for witness. We discovered that, even with the obstacles of language and culture, it's possible to establish meaningful contact quickly when we are really interested in people and genuinely want to get to know them.

The way Philip dealt with the Ethiopian eunuch still works today. As we show true interest and concern toward people, we will also be given opportunities to present the truth of the Scriptures to them and to tell them about the Lord Jesus.

Resulting Salvation

As Philip questioned the Ethiopian eunuch and explained the Scriptures to him, this devout man soon came to the place where he understood the

Gospel and trusted Jesus as his Saviour. Immediately after this he said, "See, here is water. What hinders me from being baptized?" (Acts 8:36). Note Philip's response. He didn't say, "You can't be baptized right now. You haven't been a believer long enough." Nor did he remonstrate with the eunuch by suggesting, "Maybe we should wait until we can get to some formal place of worship." On the contrary, Philip answered, "If you believe with all your heart, you may" (v. 37). To which he received the reply, "I believe that Jesus Christ is the Son of God" (v. 37). We know that this was sufficient, for the Bible then states, "And both Philip and the eunuch went down into the water, and he baptized him" (v. 38).

I love the confidence that the people in the early church placed in the power of the Gospel. They preached the message clearly. They asked for full commitment. But when they were assured that the believer had taken the necessary step of faith, they quickly received him fully into their fellowship. Their response is so much better than the skeptical "wait and see" attitude that we often demonstrate. I have an idea the eunuch probably still needed to change and rectify several areas of his life. Philip didn't insist, "Clear up all these areas first, and then you can be baptized." Being baptized doesn't certify that a person has reached Christian maturity. It's a public testimony of the fact that the believer has trusted Jesus, has received forgiveness of sins and has become identified with his Saviour in His death and resurrection.

As the eunuch continued his journey, rejoicing in his new-found salvation, the Spirit of the Lord caught Philip away (see v. 39). It's not hard to understand the first part. Everyone who has received salvation in Christ knows the great joy the eunuch felt. However, it is difficult to know why the Lord arranged for Philip to disappear so suddenly.

Why didn't the Lord allow Philip to accompany the eunuch on his journey? Evidently, the Spirit of God decided that the eunuch was able to be on his own. If we had made the decision, I believe we would have had Philip accompany the eunuch all the way back to Ethiopia to make sure he'd follow the right path. But the Lord chose to act differently. Why? Because the eunuch had the Word of God and the Spirit of God. He had everything he needed to mature in his Christian life. So much for our ideas on the great need for follow-up! Of course, this doesn't mean that we shouldn't follow up on new believers when we can; however, we must never forget that God can take care of His own people. We need to effectively share the Gospel with our unsaved friends, relatives and acquaintances, and then commit these new believers to the Lord, nurturing them with prayer and loving support.

Interesting Conclusion

At this point, the curtain falls on the life of the Ethiopian eunuch. For some reason, the Scriptures don't complete the story. We can only guess what happened to him after he returned home. However,

31

it is likely that he told Candace, the queen of Ethiopia, and others about what had happened to him. Through this eunuch, the Gospel was extended into that country.

Meanwhile, Philip was carried away by the Spirit and soon found himself at Azotus (see Acts 8:40). There he continued to evangelize, gradually making his way northward to Caesarea. Philip was not satisfied with the work he had already done. He was "ready in season and out of season" to preach the Word (II Tim. 4:2).

At this juncture in Philip's life, he moves out of the limelight and off center stage. We do catch a glimpse of him again in Acts 21:8, where he is called "the evangelist." Here we learn that he had settled in Caesarea and had four daughters who prophesied (see v. 9). From this reference, it appears that his commission from God as an evangelist continued to be valid. Therefore, I think we can safely conclude that Philip continued to serve faithfully with good results. The Bible pictures him as that kind of a man.

It does seem surprising, however, that Philip drops out of the picture so completely. When God was working with Cornelius, who lived in Caesarea, he didn't call on Philip. Instead, He called for Peter, who was in Joppa at the time. Why? Maybe Peter needed this ministry at that point in his life. Certainly the Lord taught Peter an important lesson through the experience (see Acts 10). Whatever the Lord's reasons were, from this time on, Peter and Paul become the focus of attention in the work of the Church, while Philip and others continue to serve quietly in the background.

The life of Philip teaches us, once again, that we should not be surprised if God works in a way different from what we would have chosen. No matter what God calls us to do, we need to trust Him completely and serve Him faithfully. When we follow Him in this way, our efforts will be blessed with good results.

I've worked for years with a missionary colleague whom few people in the outside world know. When I see the quality and quantity of his service for Christ, I wonder why he doesn't receive more recognition. But then I remind myself that he is doing his work quietly, humbly and effectively. Therefore, it doesn't matter that he isn't receiving the plaudits of men. The Lord recognizes how he is living and will reward him accordingly. The Bible assures me that he will receive the Saviour's "well done, good and faithful servant" (Matt. 25:21). Every servant of Christ has this certainty, even though his or her work may be unrecognized and unrewarded on earth. While we may not be in the world's spotlight, all who faithfully serve are bathed in God's light, and that is sufficient.

Chapter 3

The Power of God to Salvation
(Acts 9:1-9)

One of the most gratifying experiences a Christian can have is seeing the conversion of an "impossible" person. This kind of conversion bears testimony to the great power of God and of His Gospel.

I had a friend in Ecuador whose first name was Ecuador. I never tired of listening to him tell about God's work in his life. By Ecuador's own admission, he had lived a terribly corrupt life. Like Paul, he described himself as the "chief" of sinners. He had such a reputation for wickedness that women and children ran and hid when they heard he was in the area. Yet the Lord marvelously saved him and made him a new creature in Christ.

Nothing is too hard for God. We should never consider any person to be a hopeless case. Even the most wicked person can be transformed by the power of God's saving grace. I believe it was Charles Simeon, the great English preacher, who said that we should always remember how far the mercy of God can reach and what great things the grace of Christ can effect.

Probably no conversion experience typifies this

truth more than that of Saul of Tarsus. The grace and mercy of God transformed this fanatical persecutor into the most fervent missionary the world has ever known. The story of Saul's dramatic conversion in Acts 9 is one that will strengthen our faith in God's saving power.

Great Sin

The Book of Acts and Paul's own admissions in his epistles leave no doubt about what kind of a man he was before his conversion (see Acts 7:54-60; 22:3-21; 26:9-18). Paul called himself the "chief" of sinners (I Tim. 1:15). When we study his case, it's not hard to understand why. We first meet Saul of Tarsus at the stoning of Stephen (see Acts 7:54-60). Here we learn that "the witnesses laid down their clothes at the feet of a young man named Saul" (v. 58) and that he heartily endorsed the execution (see 8:1). Paul himself later admitted that he was "consenting to his death" (22:20).

The death of Stephen seemed to spur on Saul even more. From that point on, he became a fanatical persecutor of the Christians. The Bible tells us, "He made havoc of the church, entering every house, and dragging off men and women, committing them to prison" (8:3). Saul was so consumed with hatred and fanaticism that he began to act like a wild animal. Soon he was not content to limit his wickedness and persecution to Jerusalem. Acts 9:1,2 tells us, "Then Saul, still breathing threats and murder against the disciples of the Lord, went to the high priest and asked letters from him to the synagogues of Damascus, so that if he found any who were of the Way, whether men or women, he might bring them bound to Jerusalem." Saul obtained permission to go to Damascus, located about 130 miles northeast of Jerusalem, in order to arrest Christians and bring them captive to Jerusalem. This was a long journey in those days and shows what lengths Saul was prepared to go to in his zeal to wipe out the Church.

But merely imprisoning the Christians was not enough for this devout Jew. Paul himself declared that he "persecuted this Way to the death" (22:4). He later added, "And when they were put to death, I cast my vote against them" (26:10). Saul sincerely believed that he was accomplishing God's will by murdering many Christians.

Thus, we have a picture here of great sin. Saul wanted nothing less than to destroy the Church, and he was prepared to use any means to accomplish that purpose. Of course, he never would have succeeded. We have the Lord's promise that the gates of hell will never prevail against the Church (see Matt. 16:18).

Are people such as Saul of Tarsus impossible to save? Definitely not! The Gospel can change even the chief of sinners. I have seen the Lord work in miraculous ways through the broadcasts of Back to the Bible, HCJB and others. For example, I have a friend in Indiana who is a successful businessman and a dedicated Christian. On one occasion recently, he invited several customers to go on a fishing trip in the Canadian north woods. Before he left, he asked his wife and friends to pray for him as he shared his testimony with those unsaved customers. During the trip, he took advantage of every opportunity to tell them of the Lord Jesus. But the men showed little interest in the Gospel.

Then, after several days, the Lord provided a dramatic opening for Christian testimony. Quite unexpectedly one morning, a rugged woodsman walked into the fishing camp. He sat down and began to talk freely with the fishermen. Soon he was recounting his life story. He admitted that he had been very wicked. He said, "I had a bad reputation. I was an alcoholic and had mistreated my wife and family. I cheated everybody I could. But then something happened that changed my life. One day as I was tuning my shortwave radio, I began to listen to a station in South America called HCJB, The Voice of the Andes. They presented a message such as I had never heard before. Then one day I responded to their invitation and knelt down in my cabin and received Jesus Christ as my Saviour."

The man went on, "Jesus Christ changed my life. I have given up drinking. I treat my wife and children as I should. I now have a good reputation, and people trust me. I am a new creature."

The fishermen listened in amazement to the man's story. Their interest was aroused, and as a result, this Christian businessman was given a priceless opportunity to share Christ with them. That woodsman is just one more shining example of the fact that no person is too sinful for the Lord to save. Maybe you have some people in your life whom you have considered hopeless. Perhaps God wants you to renew your efforts to pray for them and to witness to them. Remember, if the Lord can save a Saul of Tarsus, He can save anyone.

Great Grace

As Saul approached Damascus, no doubt he was plotting ways to carry out his evil plan against the Christians. Little did he know that his life was about to change forever. Suddenly he was blinded by a brilliant light. And in that light he looked up to behold the glorious, risen Saviour (see Acts 9:3).

This appearance by the Lord Jesus in glory is one of only four recorded in the New Testament. His first appearance in this form was before His disciples on the Mount of Transfiguration (see Matt. 17:1-13; Mark 9:2-10; Luke 9:28-36). The second person to see the Saviour in His glorious body was Stephen, as he was being martyred for his faith (see Acts 7:55,56). Jesus then appeared to Saul on the Damascus road. Finally, the Apostle John saw Him in a vision on the isle of Patmos, where he was a prisoner (see Rev. 1:9-18).

As Saul fell to the ground, he heard the Saviour ask him, "Saul, Saul, why are you persecuting Me?" (Acts 9:4). When Saul questioned, "Who are You, Lord?" He responded, "I am Jesus, whom you are persecuting" (v. 5). Notice that Jesus didn't say, "Why are you persecuting My believers?" The Lord's words speak dramatically about His concern for His Church and His people. It also teaches us another tremendous truth: Persecuting a believer is

38

the same as persecuting Christ Himself. When we suffer, He suffers.

During our service as missionaries, my wife and I have often seen believers suffering persecution at the hands of enemies of the Gospel. We ourselves have suffered major attacks simply because we were preaching the message of the Lord Jesus. In such a situation, we can find great strength in the knowledge that Jesus Christ has not left us alone. He goes with us every step of the way.

Recently we heard about a new convert among the Quechua Indians of the mountains of western South America. These Indians are descendants of the Incas. This new convert was dragged by some of his former friends to a party, where they tried to force him to drink with them as he used to do. He refused, telling his friends that he had become a follower of Jesus Christ. They wouldn't take no for an answer. They seized him and forcibly tried to pour the whiskey down his throat. Then they beat him cruelly. He died as a result. The minute I heard the story, I recalled the words of Jesus, "I am Jesus, whom you are persecuting" (v. 5). Even as this dear Indian brother lay dying, our glorified Lord was there—just as He was in the case of Stephen— helping and encouraging His suffering servant.

When we are being persecuted for the Lord's sake, we know that He is suffering along with us. This is a great comfort to us. But it is also a challenge, for we can take this truth one step further. When we sin against others and even against ourselves, we are really sinning against the Lord Jesus

Christ. The opposite is also true. When we serve others in Jesus' name, we are serving the Lord Himself. "Inasmuch as you did it to one of the least of these My brethren, you did it to Me" (Matt. 25:40).

Thank God, no matter what we have done against Him, Jesus continues to be gracious. He gives us the same grace and mercy that He showed to Saul on the road to Damascus. Saul was fighting against the Lord with every ounce of his strength, yet Jesus kept on loving Saul and desiring his salvation. He tenderly told Saul, "It is hard for you to kick against the goads" (Acts 9:5).

Like an ox who was resolutely rejecting the goad, Saul was fighting vigorously against the prodding of his conscience. And he had many goads to battle. First, the death of Stephen undoubtedly made a great impression on Saul. Stephen's calmness and strength in the face of death would have shaken even a determined fanatic. Second, Saul had the testimony of the Scriptures. Of course, his understanding of them was erroneous. Nevertheless, in his most rational moments, the prophecies of the Old Testament must have caused him concern. Finally, the conduct of the Christians goaded Saul day after day. The more he fought against them, the more he saw the power and love of Jesus Christ in them. God Himself was ordering the circumstances to lead Saul to salvation. The Lord still works that way today. "The goodness of God leads you to repentance" (Rom. 2:4).

When we are tempted to become discouraged in

our efforts to witness, we should remember that many people who are fighting against God are "kicking against the goads." Even when they seem to be most opposed to the Gospel, circumstances and conditions ordered by God are pricking their consciences. God loves them and desires their salvation. Let us not grow weary in our work for the Lord. Like Saul, they will come to the place where they will cease resisting His call and will surrender to the Lord Jesus.

Great Submission

It's hard to imagine what Saul was thinking and feeling as he heard and saw the One he had been persecuting. He finally realized that Jesus Christ was no false prophet or revolutionary but was God Himself. The weight of guilt and sin must have been tremendous. Yet, he discovered that Jesus loved him just the same. The light broke through his hard heart, and Saul was finally ready to submit his life completely to Christ. He humbly asked, "Lord, what do You want me to do?" (Acts 9:6), and Jesus answered, "Arise and go into the city, and you will be told what you must do" (v. 6).

Even though our encounter with the Lord Jesus may not be as dramatic as Saul's was, we still experience salvation in the same way. First, we must recognize who Jesus is. Then we must admit our sinfulness and repent of our sins. Finally, we must accept Him as our Saviour and Lord. Once we have done this, we must then be willing to follow the Lord's orders, even when we don't know the reason

41

for doing so or what our next step will be. The true Christian abdicates the throne of his life and turns it over to the King.

Many years ago John and Betty Stam gave their lives for Christ in the land of China. In the biography of their lives, *The Triumph of John and Betty Stam,* Betty described how she surrendered her life to the Lord as a high school student. At that time, she dedicated herself to Christ completely, saying, "Lord, I give up all my own plans and purposes, all my own desires and hopes, and accept Thy will for my life. I give myself, my life, my all utterly to Thee to be Thine forever. Fill me and seal me with Thy Holy Spirit. Use me as Thou wilt; send me where Thou wilt; work out Thy whole will in my life at any cost, now and forever." What a beautiful statement! Every person who belongs to the Lord Jesus should also express in word and in action this same kind of devotion. It's the least we can do for the One who gave everything for us!

When Jesus had finished speaking, Saul opened his eyes and discovered that he couldn't see. He followed the Lord's instructions and had his companions lead him into Damascus. For the next three days, Saul lived in total darkness, refusing to eat or drink anything. But the Bible gives no indication that Saul was anxious or depressed. After his dramatic encounter with Jesus, Saul knew that the Lord was in control, so he didn't need to be worried or frustrated. He was sure that His glorified Lord knew what He was doing. Therefore, he could afford to wait.

Those three days must have been very special for Saul. Imagine what he was thinking! He must have thought, first of all, about how glorious and wonderful Jesus is. Saul's physical eyes could not see, but he must have seen the vision of his Saviour many times during that time. He later described the Lord's grace and glory in his epistles. During those first three days, Saul's attitude changed as he experienced the love and beauty of the Saviour.

Then Saul probably reflected on his past sin and foolishness. His heart ached as he recalled the many people he had killed, imprisoned and caused to suffer because of his fanaticism. He confessed these sins to the Lord Jesus and experienced the cleansing power of His blood. No doubt he must have wavered at times, asking himself, *Can I really be forgiven for the terrible sins I have committed?* I'm sure that the Devil accused this forgiven sinner repeatedly during this time, trying to cause him to doubt the salvation and forgiveness he had received. But Saul had discovered the truth of I John 1:7: "The blood of Jesus Christ His Son cleanses us from all sin."

Finally, Saul probably considered how he could serve Jesus. He had been Satan's slave for a long time. Now he was impatient to see action in the Lord's army. He may have wondered if he could witness effectively in the places where he had previously assaulted Christians. He knew that it would be hard, but he was willing to suffer for his faith, just as other believers had. Subsequent events showed just how ready Saul was to serve.

Saul's life demonstrates to us that no sin is too great to be forgiven, no sinner is too hopeless to be saved, when God's grace and mercy leads that person to the place of repentance and submission. When we consider what the Lord did for Saul and others like him, we stand amazed at the goodness and grace of God and at the power of His Gospel. More than ever, we should want to share this message with those around us. The Gospel changed Saul of Tarsus, and it can change many others also, when we obey Christ's command to go and preach.

Chapter 4

The Power of God for Service
(Acts 9:10-22)

God frequently uses the most unlikely people to accomplish His greatest tasks. The account of Saul's conversion in Acts 9 serves as a vibrant illustration of this. Saul's encounter with the Lord Jesus on the road to Damascus led him to a place of repentance and submission. His three days of blindness prepared him for further instruction about Christ and the Christian life. Saul's conversion was probably the most important event in the life of the early church. We would think that the Lord would have sent Peter, John or Philip to restore Saul's sight and encourage him. Instead, God chose Ananias, an unknown believer, and gave him the honor of performing this wonderful service in Saul's life. And Saul, the former persecutor, would become one of the most powerful preachers the world has ever known. Indeed, God uses unlikely people!

The example of Ananias and Saul shows us that God can use and bless every believer, provided we yield to Him and allow His power to flow through us. As a missionary, I have had the joyous privilege of seeing the Lord take simple and unlearned people and do great things through them. Two men, both named Jaime, illustrate this truth.

The first Jaime suffered from an advanced case of tuberculosis. During his illness, he heard the Gospel and became a true believer. He prayed that God would raise him up from his sickbed and give him the opportunity to witness to many people. The Lord honored his request. For almost two years Jaime had the energy and strength to walk the streets of Quito, Ecuador, and the surrounding counties to share his faith with many fellow citizens. Then he was forced to return to his sickbed, and he died shortly thereafter. I was present in Jaime's small room when he passed from this life into Christ's presence. All of us in that room thanked God for the remarkable way in which He had used Jaime during those two years. In that short time, this faithful man probably witnessed to more people than most of us will in a lifetime.

The other Jaime lived in a very fanatical town north of Quito. He and his family suffered great persecution. On a number of occasions Jaime joined me in a Gospel sound truck ministry. I will always remember our prayer times. Often Jaime prayed so fervently that he fell to the floor, and with his face to the ground, he cried out to God. He demonstrated great courage in the open air Gospel meetings. His ardor convicted me. Like Ananias, Jaime illustrated how beautifully God can fill a simple person with His power.

Ananias and the Lord

Who was Ananias, and why did God choose to use him in bringing physical and spiritual sight to

46

Saul? The Bible tells us very little about this man. He only appears in this passage and in Paul's address to the Jerusalem mob as he recounts the experience (see Acts 22:12-16). From Paul's account, we learn that Ananias faithfully followed the Law and that he had a good testimony among the Jews in Damascus (see v. 12). Undoubtedly he had come to faith in Jesus as the Messiah, or he would not have been chosen by the Lord for this important assignment with Saul.

Why did the Lord choose Ananias? Because he was open and willing to be used. As we read Acts 9, the one characteristic of Ananias that immediately stands out is his spirit of submission and obedience to Jesus. When the Lord spoke to him in a vision, Ananias immediately replied, "Here I am, Lord" (v. 10). Like Abraham, Joseph, Samuel and other faithful servants before him, Ananias was ready and willing to listen to the Lord's commands and obey them.

Of course, Ananias experienced the same feelings we often do when we are called to perform a difficult task. When he heard what his job was going to be, he remonstrated some with the Lord. He stated, "Lord, I have heard from many about this man, how much harm he has done to Your saints in Jerusalem" (v. 13). Ananias feared for his life. He was also no doubt confused about the Lord's reasons for wanting to heal the man who had persecuted so many believers. But notice Ananias's response after Jesus explained His intentions to

47

him. The Lord told Ananias, "Go, for he is a chosen vessel of Mine to bear My name before Gentiles, kings, and the children of Israel" (v. 15). The Bible then adds, "And Ananias went his way and entered the house" (v. 17). He did not delay or make excuses; he set out immediately to obey God's directions. The response of Ananias shows us that it is not wrong to have doubts or fears as we serve, as long as these do not keep us from obeying the Lord's will.

However, all too often we delay in carrying out the Lord's will. We are like children when they are told to go to bed. Instead of obeying the clear instructions of their parents, children will use every strategy they can think of to delay it, from needing a drink of water to requiring another trip to the bathroom or wanting an answer to an urgent question. In the same way, we as God's children frequently run from Him or make excuses when we are called to serve. Then, after the Lord has prodded us for some time, we finally give reluctant obedience. But this falls far short of the immediate and willing obedience that Ananias exhibited. Being a willing servant is so much better than having to be forced into obedience. When we delay, we frequently miss many of the blessings that would have come from our service.

The Lord told Ananias that Saul was His chosen vessel to the Gentiles (see v. 15). And Ananias was the vessel God used to take this message to Saul. We can be a usable vessel also if we will submit to the Master Potter and allow Him to shape and mold us according to the image of Jesus Christ. Then we will be vessels of honor "sanctified and useful for the Master, prepared for every good work" (II Tim. 2:21). This does not mean that God will call every believer to be a world-famous evangelist. Romans 9:21 tells us that God molds us according to His will. Some vessels are destined to be viewed by all; others are designed for common use. But each is equally important. The ministry of Ananias was just as important as that of Saul, for if Ananias had not completed his task, Saul might never have regained his sight or received his calling to preach. Even though we may be simple earthen vessels, we can be the bearers of God's power and glory when we allow His Spirit to fill and use us (see II Cor. 4:7).

Because he was ready and willing to serve, Ananias was given the tremendous task of commissioning the great apostle to the Gentiles. I'm sure that in his wildest dreams Ananias never imagined that he would be called to a mission of that magnitude. But as we have seen, God often chooses humble and unknown people to do some of His greatest work. I'm reminded of that fact every time I read about the life and witness of William Carey, the father of the modern missionary movement. Who would have thought that a simple cobbler with no obvious gifts could have become the great missionary pioneer and statesman that God made him? And he is just one of many examples of what the Lord can do with someone who is open to His leading. Therefore, let's be ready to respond when God calls us, knowing that when He commissions us for a task, He also provides the resources to accomplish it.

Ananias and Saul

True obedience to God is measured not only by our *actions* but also by our *attitude* as we serve. Ananias's willingness to go immediately to the house where Saul was staying is commendable; however, his attitude after he arrived is even more remarkable. Upon entering the house, Ananias laid his hands on Saul and said, "Brother Saul, the Lord Jesus, who appeared to you on the road as you came, has sent me that you may receive your sight and be filled with the Holy Spirit" (Acts 9:17). Ananias could have been suspicious of Saul or could have taken advantage of Saul's blindness to retaliate in behalf of all the Christians who had been persecuted by Saul. Instead, Ananias showed overflowing Christian love and forgiveness toward Saul. He considered him to be his brother in Christ and was willing to see him receive the gift of the Holy Spirit.

Some time ago I traveled to the islands of Fiji for a radio consultation. There I met a Muslim woman who had accepted Christ. This woman told me about her sister, who had suffered horrible disfigurement when a jilted lover threw acid into her face while she was sleeping. As she told me the story, I noticed a complete absence of hate and resentment. Not only did she feel great compassion for her sister, but she expressed a loving concern for the man who had hurt her sister so much. She longed to see him come to repentance and faith in the Lord Jesus. Because this woman was being controlled by God, she was able to express this kind of Christian love.

As Ananias laid his hands on Saul and gave him the Lord's message, four things took place. First, Saul regained his sight (see v. 18). He was no doubt greatly relieved when he could see again, although he probably was willing to remain blind if this had been the Lord's will. Those three sightless days had left an indelible impression on the new convert's heart and had taught him lessons he might not have learned otherwise. Second, Saul was filled with the Holy Spirit. The restoration of his physical sight typified the larger spiritual vision that Saul received by the indwelling of the Holy Spirit.

Immediately after this, Saul arose and was baptized (see v. 18). No good reason existed to delay the baptism. He had definitely received the Lord as his Saviour. The Holy Spirit had filled him. It was most appropriate that he be baptized without delay. This leads me to point out once more that the Christians in Acts did not exhibit faithless caution. They believed in God's power to change people. When the person professed his faith in Jesus Christ and testified to that fact, then the other believers baptized him in total acceptance and trust.

The fourth thing that happened was that Saul received food and was strengthened (see v. 19). I find it noteworthy that the Scriptures add this very human touch. The Bible never ignores, slights or belittles the commonplace in our lives. Our Lord recognizes our daily physical needs and has taught us to pray, "Give us this day our daily bread" (Matt. 6:11). Throughout God's Word, we see this meshing of the physical and spiritual. Jesus frequently met people's physical needs for healing, nutrition and comfort before He gave them the Word of Life.

Today, as we take the Gospel to the ends of the earth, we must do so with the understanding that men and women have physical needs along with the spiritual. Certainly they need the Bread of Life above all else. But that doesn't eliminate their need for physical help. I thank God that Christian workers have taken the lead in reaching out to meet the material needs of starving and suffering people.

Saul and the Synagogues

Following his conversion, Saul spent some time with the disciples at Damascus (see Acts 9:19). Although it is not expressed directly, we can conclude that these believers gave him a warm welcome. Like Ananias, they were thankful for God's miraculous work of grace in the life of the man who had been their greatest enemy.

But Saul was not content merely to sit back and fellowship with the believers in Damascus. Like most new believers, he was eager to serve. The Bible tells us, "Immediately he preached the Christ in the synagogues, that He is the Son of God" (v. 20). Notice the twofold emphasis—Jesus is the Christ (the promised Messiah) and the Son of God. When the Jews in the synagogues heard Saul, they were amazed and said, "Isn't this the fierce persecutor? Isn't he the one who destroyed those who proclaimed the name of Jesus? Now look, he is preaching their same message!" (see v. 21).

I see two tremendous lessons in this story. First, even as new believers, God equips us for the work of witness. Saul would soon receive further training in the Lord's school for the larger task that awaited him. But from the beginning, God allowed him to witness effectively. While new believers often lack biblical knowledge, they can nevertheless have a powerful testimony as they tell others of what the Lord has done in their lives.

The second truth is that continuing effectiveness depends upon spiritual growth and maturity. We cannot have a good ongoing ministry if we continue to be spiritual babies. Our witness will have validity only as we move forward in the Christian life and exhibit the wonderful fruit of the Spirit. Saul could serve powerfully as a new Christian, but he needed to delve deeper into God's truth in order to serve the Lord and others on a continuing basis.

Saul undoubtedly realized this as well, for after he left Damascus, he went off by himself to receive God's preparation for future service. In Galatians 1:17, he informed us, "Nor did I go up to Jerusalem to those who were apostles before me; but I went to Arabia and returned again to Damascus." Saul still had a great deal to learn. Before he could present himself for service to the other apostles in Jerusalem, he needed to attend God's school of solitude, meditation, Bible study and communion with the Lord. The three days of solitude right after his conversion helped Saul a great deal, but he needed the time in Arabia even more. Saul's subsequent ministry depended greatly upon that time away from active ministry in public. God was preparing Saul for worldwide outreach.

We find this same pattern throughout the Old and New Testaments. The Lord spent a great deal of time and attention preparing His servants for ministry. He spent 40 years preparing Moses in the desert before sending him back to Egypt. And the Lord Himself fasted 40 days in the desert before embarking on His public ministry. In addition, He spent more than three years preparing His disciples for their great work. He did not send His men into battle without the proper spiritual "basic training." The Bible instructs us, "Do not lay hands on anyone hastily" (I Tim. 5:22). Many times we tend to forget this as we try to rush celebrity converts onto the public stage or to push people into vacant places of service because the need is great. Saul took time to let God prepare him for well-grounded service, and we should do the same.

I believe that Acts 9:22 refers to Saul's ministry after his return from Arabia. While he had preached with power right after his conversion, he was testifying now with even greater power. The Bible tells us that he had "increased all the more in strength" (v. 22). Furthermore, Saul confounded the Jews who opposed the message and convincingly proved to them that Jesus was the Christ. The extra time of preparation he had received in Arabia enabled him to deliver God's message to the resistant Jews bravely and wisely. Saul's listeners were amazed, not only at his spiritual maturity but also at the message he preached. They couldn't believe that this was the same man who formerly had persecuted Jesus Christ and His Church with every ounce of his strength. As they saw the change that had taken place in him, Saul no doubt had the joy and privilege of leading some of his companions in wickedness to the feet of Jesus Christ where they, too, could surrender their lives to Him.

The life of Ananias shows us that God uses ordinary people to accomplish extraordinary tasks when they allow Him to control and use them. The only requirement is a willingness to obey. In the life of Saul, we see how the grace and power of the Lord Jesus can transform even the greatest sinner into an effective servant. Saul's ministry also shows us the importance of allowing the Lord to prepare us for the work He has for us. We need times of solitude, meditation, study and communion with Him in prayer in order to be equipped for an ongoing ministry. Today, Christ's army desperately needs soldiers like Ananias and Saul—believers who are willing to step out in obedience and take the Gospel even to our worst enemies. He needs soldiers who have readied themselves for battle in His spiritual boot camp of study and prayer. May we be this kind of soldiers.

Chapter 5

The Power of God to Protect and Prosper
(Acts 9:23-31)

In Acts 9 we see the Church being equipped for larger service. We observe this first in God's continuing preparation of a unique individual for widespread service. At this point, we find Saul entering an adventurous career that continued unabated until he became a prisoner for the Gospel in Rome. Even there he was actively involved in witness, and he wrote important epistles during that time. In addition, we see God's equipping power displayed in the growth that the Church was experiencing, both in times of persecution and of peace.

Foiled Plot

Saul, the persecutor, soon became Saul, the persecuted, as he boldly began to share his newfound faith among his Jewish friends in Damascus. After his return from Arabia, Saul entered the synagogues and powerfully preached to the Jews gathered there. Try as they might, the Jews couldn't provide answers for Saul's arguments concerning Jesus Christ. Saul's zeal and reason confounded them, and they couldn't compete with the power of the Holy Spirit that flowed from him (see Acts 9:22). So they did the only thing they could think of to stop him—they devised a plot to kill him (see v. 23). "But their plot became known to Saul" (v. 24). God's protecting hand was on Saul. The Lord somehow warned Saul of the murderous plot against him and enabled the apostle to elude their grasp.

This was just the first of many incidents in which the Lord worked in Paul's behalf so he could continue his ministry. In Acts 23 Paul's enemies were again plotting to kill him. This time Paul's nephew heard of their ambush and warned him in time (see vv. 11-16). Time and time again, Paul's enemies were foiled in their efforts to silence him. What they didn't know was that they couldn't touch him until God allowed them to do so. No matter how secretive or clever the plans of wicked people may be, these plans will not succeed unless God in His sovereignty allows them to do so. The Lord knows and can thwart any and every plot that unbelievers devise to damage His people. Thus, we can be assured that God will protect us according to His perfect will as we serve Him.

Jesus testified to this truth during His ministry on earth. One day the Pharisees came to Him and warned Him, "Get out and depart from here, for Herod wants to kill You" (Luke 13:31). But Jesus didn't run or hide. Instead, He told them, "Go, tell that fox, 'Behold, I cast out demons and perform cures today and tomorrow, and the third day I shall be perfected' " (v. 32). Despite Herod's plans to kill Him, Jesus knew He would carry out His God-given

57

schedule until He had completed His work. Then, and only then, would He lay down His life for mankind, using His enemies to accomplish His purposes.

David Livingstone knew the truth of the Lord's words. He once stated, "I lead a charmed life. My life is charmed until my work for God is done." This does not mean that the Lord will not call us to suffer or even to die for our faith. But we can be assured that if and when He does, it will be in accordance with His plan for our lives.

In my many years of missionary service, I have seen God's protection displayed again and again in the lives of believers. Small groups of Christians have successfully stood against the overwhelming majority, who were determined to eliminate them. I have witnessed how the Lord has led many of these people through the fire to safety and security. From time to time, I have even heard of dramatic and miraculous divine interventions.

In the mountains of southern Ecuador, a small group of Quechua Indians had accepted the Lord and were living and witnessing for Him. They were facing fierce opposition from the other Indians in the area. One day several of these opponents gathered to discuss what they could do to stop this Gospel movement. They decided that if they could kill the ringleader of the group, then the other believers would probably stop witnessing. So they made plans to meet on a certain day to surround the believer's home and murder him. As the men gathered on the designated day, they first stopped at a local tavern and drank profusely to gather courage for their violent act. Then they set out for the Christian's house. When they drew near, they saw that the house was surrounded by a large group of Ecuadorean soldiers. They all looked several times but saw the same thing. Frustrated and thwarted, they returned to their homes without laying a hand on the believer.

A few days later, these men found the believer and asked him, "How did you know we were going to kill you? Where did you get all those soldiers? We didn't know you had that kind of government influence." The Christian told the men that he knew nothing about their plot, nor had he seen any soldiers surrounding his house. Just as the Lord protected Elisha (see II Kings 6:13-17), it appears that He sent His host of angels to encamp around that humble house and deliver His servant.

Saul managed to avoid his enemies in Damascus for some time. Galatians 1:18 tells us that Saul didn't go to Jerusalem until three years after his conversion. Except for the time he spent in Arabia preparing for his ministry, he remained in Damascus, preaching in the synagogues and fellowshipping with the believers. But opposition to his ministry gradually intensified. The Jews began plotting to kill him. They placed guards at the gates of the city so he could not escape and then looked for an opportunity to capture him.

As the situation worsened, the disciples devised a plan to help Saul escape. Damascus, like many ancient cities, was surrounded by huge walls. The walls were often so wide that chariots could drive on them. Frequently, houses were built into these walls. They often had windows that were built into the outer wall itself and gave a view of the surrounding countryside. So one night the disciples evidently smuggled Saul into a house and then let him out through a window in a large basket (see Acts 9:25; II Cor. 11:32,33).

Try to picture this scene. What a humbling way of making an escape! But Saul was willing to endure any humiliation or hardship for the sake of serving his Saviour. We can learn two important lessons from Saul's experience. First, we see that even though God will often intervene and foil the plots of men, this doesn't mean that we should behave fool-hardily. Rather than playing the martyr and allowing his enemies to kill him, Saul used human means to escape from Damascus. He didn't place himself in a situation where the Lord would be forced to perform a miracle to rescue him. In an age when missionaries face grave dangers working in areas of violence and unrest, we would do well to remember Saul's example. Although we should be willing to die for our faith if necessary, we should nevertheless exercise reasonable precautions whenever possible.

Second, we see in Saul's experience a great example of forgiveness on the part of the believers in Damascus. The disciples who facilitated Saul's escape were the same people Saul had originally come to imprison and murder. But they had accepted Saul's conversion as genuine. Since their Lord had forgiven him, they were able to forgive him also. I'm sure that, as Saul made his way from

Damascus to Jerusalem, his heart overflowed with joy and gratitude for those Christian disciples who had received him warmly and served as his protectors. Do we today show the same compassion and forgiveness toward our enemies when they come to Christ?

Friendly Protector

Saul received a far different reception in Jerusalem from the one he had enjoyed in Damascus. Acts 9:26 tells us, "And when Saul had come to Jerusalem, he tried to join the disciples; but they were all afraid of him, and did not believe that he was a disciple." The disciples in Jerusalem gave Saul the cold shoulder. They feared him, and many didn't believe he was a disciple. Some believers suspected that Saul's change in attitude was only a ploy to trap them.

This experience must have been Saul's greatest trial to that point. He could accept the persecution he was receiving from his enemies. He could even understand why the disciples were afraid and suspicious. Nevertheless, he longed to be accepted by them and wondered why they wouldn't rejoice with him over his new life in Christ.

At this difficult juncture, Barnabas came to the rescue. He befriended Saul and testified to the genuineness of Saul's faith. He took Saul to the apostles and had him relate the story of his conversion (see v. 27). What a tremendous spirit Barnabas displayed here and in other circumstances! Once again Barnabas demonstrated why he had earned the name "Son of Encouragement" (see 4:36). With his cordial nature and his spiritual intuition, Barnabas could recognize what the others had failed to see. Concerning this incident, William Barclay wrote: "First, the Church owed Paul to the prayer of Stephen. Then the Church owed Paul to the forgiving spirit of Ananias. Now we see the Church owing Paul to the large-hearted charity of Barnabas. . . . By this action Barnabas showed himself to be a really Christian man. (i) He was a man who insisted on believing the best of others. . . . (ii) He was a man who never held anyone's past against him" (*The Acts of the Apostles,* pp. 75,76).

From Paul's letters we learn something of his activities during this visit to Jerusalem. He spent some quality time with the leaders there. Besides his friendship with Barnabas, we learn that Saul spent 15 days with Peter (see Gal. 1:18). He also met with James, the brother of Jesus and leader of the church in Jerusalem (see v. 19). No doubt these three men were a great blessing and help to Saul at that time. I wish I could have been present at these gatherings and heard their conversations and prayers. The Lord was continuing to prepare Saul for the work that lay ahead. Likewise, God was instructing the other leaders through the remarkable conversion of Saul. Their faith in the power of God must have increased as they personally observed the transformation that had taken place in Saul's life.

In Jerusalem as well as in Damascus, Saul spoke boldly in the name of the Lord Jesus. The Bible specifically tells us that he disputed against the Hel-

lenists, the non-Palestinian Jews (Acts 9:29).
Stephen had exercised a special ministry with them.
Now Saul was doing the same. How wonderful are
the ways of God! The very man who took part in
Stephen's execution and heartily consented to his
death was now carrying on the ministry he had
begun.

Like Stephen, Saul faced opposition from the
Hellenists. Once again he was in danger of being
killed by his enemies, and he was forced to leave.
Just as the Lord had thwarted the plans of the
enemies in Damascus, he again enabled Saul to
escape from his enemies in Jerusalem. Saul's Christian friends helped him get to Caesarea and then on
to Tarsus, his home city. We don't hear any more
about Saul until Barnabas takes him to Antioch,
where their services were needed (see 11:19-26).

Already Saul was beginning to stand out from the
other apostles in his work among the Gentiles. As
time went on, his role as apostle to the Gentiles
became even more pronounced. The fact that the
Lord selected Saul for a wide-ranging mission to the
Gentiles is vivid proof of how God chooses the right
people for specific tasks. He matches our talents
and experience with the areas where we can best
serve. Saul had unique qualifications that made him
the perfect person for the task. First, he was a true
Hebrew. He had studied under the finest Jewish
teacher of the day, Gamaliel, and knew the Scriptures well. And unlike the other apostles, Saul had
grown up in a Hellenistic culture in Tarsus (see
22:3). Finally, he was a Roman citizen (see

63

vv. 27,28). This stood him in good stead with many of the Gentiles and saved his life on several occasions. All three of these factors prepared him uniquely for his God-appointed mission.

Sometimes we tend to place Paul on a pedestal and to think that no one could be used the way he was. But we don't have to look at Paul longingly from a distance and say, "I wish that God would work that way with me." The Lord still takes the gifts and backgrounds He has given us and fits us into the areas of service where we can honor Him the most. We must simply be willing to accept His guidance and to step obediently into the ministry He calls us to do. We can find no greater joy in our Christian life than that of living and working in the sanctified place that God has appointed for us.

Further Prospering

In Acts 9:31 we find another update of the situation in the early church. The church was continuing to grow and prosper greatly. What was the secret of their growth? In this passage we discover four important facts about the believers that were at the heart of their success. When today's churches begin to follow their example in these areas, then we will also begin to see great things happen.

Their Featured Fellowship

In the best texts and translations, Acts 9:31 begins, "Then the church throughout all Judea, Galilee and Samaria." There were various congregations in different places, but the church was one.

Thank God that even such different people as those of Judea, Galilee and Samaria became one through the powerful work of the Gospel. We cannot find a better way to praise God than to practice the unity that the Gospel brings. Ephesians 4:13 reminds us, "Till we all come to the unity of the faith and the knowledge of the Son of God, to a perfect man, to the measure of the stature of the fullness of Christ."

Their Profiting From Peace and Rest

Second, we notice that the believers "had peace and were edified." The Christians of Judea, Galilee and Samaria had been suffering terrible persecution. When they at last enjoyed a time of peace, they realized that it was a gift from God. They wisely used this period of peace to grow stronger in their Christian lives. They took advantage of spiritual good weather to prepare for the difficult storms ahead. They didn't forget God in the days of peace and quiet.

I always admire those Christian brothers and sisters who are prosperous but who, at the same time, maintain a spirit of true devotion. The more blessings they receive, the more they thank God. One Christian businessman I know is a good example of this. He has enjoyed much success in business. His life has been relatively free from problems. But he has never taken any credit for his success; he has always given God the glory. In days of peace, he has continued to be edified.

Unfortunately, too many believers and churches do not profit from the peace they enjoy. Instead of

65

continuing to edify each other, they grow lazy and complacent. They stop working for the Lord and growing in their spiritual lives. But Amos 6:1 warns us, "Woe to you who are at ease in Zion." It's a sad but true fact that the Lord frequently has to send us through the fire in order to set us on fire for Him.

Their Obedient Outreach

Not only did the believers use their time of peace to edify one another, but they worked even harder taking the Gospel to the unsaved. Acts 9:31 tells us they were "walking in the fear of the Lord and in the comfort of the Holy Spirit." One translator renders this passage, "Going on its way in the fear of the Lord." The Greek word translated "walking" carries with it the idea of purpose. Jesus used this same root word in the Great Commission when He gave the directive, "Go therefore and make disciples of all the nations" (Matt. 28:19). Thus, these believers were keeping the goal of evangelism and outreach clearly before their eyes. They did not become satisfied with what had already been accomplished but worked even harder to carry out the missionary mandate of the Lord Jesus. Consequently, they remained alive, vital and dynamic. Their example constitutes a great challenge for us today. At no other time in history has the need for the Gospel been so great. Billions of people are dying spiritually. Unfortunately, many believers have lost sight of the goal; therefore, our arm of outreach is very short.

The reason the believers were so successful in

carrying out the Great Commission was because they did it in "the fear of the Lord and the comfort of the Holy Spirit." They stood in awe and reverence of God and His greatness. When they considered what He had done for them, they desired to serve Him all the more. In addition, they had the resources of the Holy Spirit from which to draw strength. They knew He was always near and thus were encouraged. It's important that we remember both aspects of God's personality—His greatness and His nearness. Remembering who God is and who we are will keep us from becoming too proud. We see these seemingly contradictory truths—that a God who is so great has chosen to dwell in us—stated again by the Prophet Isaiah: "I dwell in the high and holy place with him who has a contrite and humble spirit" (Isa. 57:15).

Their Good Growth

The fourth fact we learn about the believers is that "they were multiplied." A praising church doesn't stand still. Life brings growth. However, this doesn't mean that the local church must become a megachurch. It might do better by planting daughter churches. But we must remember that multiplication is a law of life. The living congregation makes an impact on its own members, its community and people everywhere. The members of such a congregation permeate their society with the Gospel and minister to the needs of people. Those churches who do not multiply will soon die.

On several occasions I visited a congregation in

67

southern South America that fits the description of Acts 9:31. Before the evening service, the members of this congregation would hold open air meetings in nearby parks. When those meetings were finished, the lay preachers would invite their listeners to follow them to church. It was quite a sight to watch the groups converging on the church from all directions. When the people had gathered, the members of this congregation would begin with an exciting praise service. Then the people would hear challenging messages from the Word of God. After the service the members would gather at different spots in the church so their leaders could give them their evangelistic assignments for the week. In another area of the church, leaders would be taking requests for help for needy people. This congregation pulsated with life. The group was growing. Like the people of the early church, they were "going on their way" in obedience to the command of Christ. They were living Acts 9:31 all over again. God help us to do the same.

Chapter 6

The Power of God in Action
(Acts 9:32-43)

The Book of Acts teaches us a beautiful and important lesson about the Holy Spirit: *He works through people in many different ways.* Jesus was referring to this variety when He stated, "The wind blows where it wishes, and you hear the sound of it, but cannot tell where it comes from and where it goes. So is everyone who is born of the Spirit" (John 3:8). By this Jesus didn't mean that the Spirit works capriciously. Instead, the Lord was calling attention to the creativity of the Holy Spirit. When unhindered, He ministers in refreshing ways through the people of God.

The Holy Spirit provides a great variety of gifts to those whom He indwells (see Rom. 12:3-8; Eph. 4:7-16; I Cor. 12:1—14:40). Therefore, we should not try to press His work into our predetermined boxes. Rather, we should continually thank God for the variety we observe in the work of the Holy Spirit. The account before us in Acts 9 serves as a good illustration of this Spirit-directed variety.

Peter's Service

As we read the Book of Acts, we are impressed by the untiring service of Peter and others. They

69

were continually on the move, taking the Gospel to every village and country. In Acts 9:32 we read this description of Peter: "Peter went through all parts of the country." He didn't feel his work was done until every city in that country had been given a chance to hear the Gospel. As a result, the church was growing by leaps and bounds!

Unfortunately, many Christians today have the strange idea that we can carry out the Great Commission without moving. But it doesn't work that way. We will never reach the lost by sitting with our arms folded, waiting for the unsaved to come to us. Take a lesson from those early disciples. They didn't let the grass grow under their feet. They knew that time was short and the task was tremendous. They earnestly used every opportunity to share the Word of God.

Of course, this doesn't mean that we should become so wrapped up in working for God that we do not take any time to fellowship with Him. However, both in the Gospels and in the Book of Acts, we observe intense, vigorous activity on the part of God's people. If we find ourselves so busy with other activities that we have no time for witnessing, then we no doubt need to rearrange our priorities.

As Peter traveled throughout Judea and Samaria, he may have been following up on the ministry that Philip had begun. In the spirit of cooperation that existed in the early church, it would have been natural for him to do so.

One of Peter's stops was at Lydda, located northwest of Jerusalem. There he met a paralytic named Aeneas, who had been confined to bed for eight years. Peter told him, "Aeneas, Jesus the Christ heals you. Arise and make your bed" (v. 34). Immediately Aeneas got up and walked. Notice that Peter gave full credit to the Lord Jesus and His power. No one can work that kind of miracle by himself. Jesus must do it, and we must give Him the credit. When the people saw the Lord's power displayed in such a dramatic way, many of them believed in Him (see v. 35).

Peter faced a greater challenge at Joppa (see vv. 38-42). While he was in Lydda, two messengers came to him and begged him to come to Joppa at once (see v. 38). Joppa, a small village on the Mediterranean coast, was located about ten miles northwest of Lydda. Dorcas, a beloved widow in the church, had become sick and died. Her friends had gathered for her burial. Peter left immediately for Joppa with the messengers. When he arrived, he was taken to the upper room where the body of Dorcas lay. He asked everyone to leave the room, and then he knelt down and prayed. When he had finished, he turned to the body and said, "Tabitha [Dorcas], arise" (v. 40). The woman opened her eyes at once and sat up. Once again, when people saw the great miracle that had taken place, many believed in Jesus, and Peter was given even more opportunities for witness.

We see great similarities here with the way that Jesus raised Jairus's daughter (see Mark 5:22-24, 35-43). The apostles had spent so much time in precious communion with their Lord that they naturally talked and acted like Him in many ways. In addition, they now had the Holy Spirit dwelling in them, who was conforming them to the image of Christ. As a result, when people saw what Peter did, they immediately recognized the source—Jesus Christ. Likewise, when we allow the Holy Spirit to work in us, people will see the image of Christ in us and will be drawn to the Saviour.

These miracles performed by Peter in the name of Jesus raise some interesting questions. First, I find myself asking, "Why was Dorcas raised and not Stephen?" While we don't have a definitive answer, we can venture a guess as to the Lord's reasons. Apparently Stephen's work was finished, while the Lord still had a continuing mission for Dorcas on earth. God, in His wisdom and sovereignty, always knows what is best. When He takes one of His children at a time that seems premature to us, then we can know without a doubt that, in God's plan, this servant's work on earth was finished. Likewise, when He snatches some of us from the brink of death, then obviously He still has more for us to do.

This story of miraculous healing raises another important question: "What about healing the sick and raising the dead today? Should Christians be doing this?" Of course, most—if not all—of us have never seen anyone directly raised from the dead. Some of us have seen what we would consider to be divine healings, although we may differ on the methods used. This leads us to ask, "Do the servants of Jesus still have the power or the gift to perform such miracles today?" We must look to the

Lord and His Word for the answer to this question.

As we consider this question, we must first realize that the specific office of apostle, established by Jesus, does not continue today. This office was confined to the 12 men appointed by Jesus, to Matthias (who replaced Judas) and to the Apostle Paul. They filled a unique role in the launching of the Church after Jesus' ascension into heaven. The fact that they did certain dramatic and miraculous works during their ministries does not mean that we are commanded and authorized to do the same. In the early days of Christianity, the believers did not have the written revelation of the New Testament. Thus, they needed a special validation. The miracles that the apostles performed in the name of Jesus provided this validation of the Gospel.

However, this doesn't mean that the Lord has ceased to perform miracles through believers today. He can, and does, perform the miraculous when it is needed to advance the Gospel. We see proof of this particularly in areas where the Gospel is entering for the first time. I have seen and heard of many amazing and miraculous acts of God in various parts of the world. Therefore, Christ's promise still applies to us today: "Most assuredly, I say to you, he who believes in Me, the works that I do he will do also; and greater works than these he will do, because I go to My Father" (John 14:12).

The Holy Spirit who lives in us has not changed. He still gives wonderful gifts to the servants of Christ. However, He only performs miracles when they are needed, and the need for such signs is not as great today. But even if the Lord does not work in the same way He did through the apostles, He will nevertheless furnish all that is needed to minister effectively in His name. I agree with the observation of G. Campbell Morgan on this matter. He stated, "The Church to-day has gifts that she had not in the apostolic age. She had gifts in the apostolic age that she has not now. . . . If He [Holy Spirit] does not to-day bestow certain gifts, He is always bestowing some. Let us take the gifts He gives, and use them, and not sigh for other gifts that are withheld in wisdom. This is the age of the Spirit. We are to act, not in imitation of the methods of the apostolic age, but in obedience to the present work and power of the Holy Spirit" (*The Acts of the Apostles*, p. 259).

Because Peter was willing to serve, the Lord used him to perform miracles in His name. At the same time, Jesus was accomplishing an even greater miracle in Peter's heart. It was not as visible as the other works, but it was no less dramatic. The chapter closes with the simple statement that Peter stayed many days in Joppa in the home of Simon, a tanner (Acts 9:43). What is so miraculous about this? It reveals a drastic change in Peter's attitudes regarding the Jewish customs. Tanners were despised by the Jews because of their profession. Since they worked with the skins of dead animals, they were considered to be unclean. The Jews did not associate directly with tanners and forced them to locate their shops outside the city. Ordinarily, Peter never would have stayed in the home of a tanner. But God was slowly showing him that the old order was passing away and that it was being fulfilled in the new. Very soon Peter would have an experience that would convince him of this truth once and for all. The Lord was patiently preparing Peter for that great event. He was leading his servant step by step to the place He wanted him. God continues to do the same today. He patiently teaches us the truths of His Word day by day, even when we need to relearn the lessons many times.

Dorcas's Example

While the Lord sometimes chooses to perform miracles through a believer, as He did in the case of Peter, often He works through us in much simpler— yet just as important—ways. The life of Dorcas is a case in point. We meet her in Acts 9 when Peter raised her from the dead, but we hear no more about her after that. However, in this short passage, we learn a great deal about this woman. We learn that she was known by both her Hebrew name, Tabitha, and its Greek equivalent, Dorcas, both of which mean "gazelle." The Bible describes her as a woman "full of good works and charitable deeds which she did" (v. 36). She really believed in loving her neighbor as herself. She dedicated a great deal of time and energy to helping others, using the abilities the Lord had given her.

The widows in the area were the primary recipients of Dorcas's caring service. She was greatly loved by these widows and the other believers in Joppa. When she became sick and died, they sent at once for Peter, hoping that he could help her.

When the apostle arrived, the Bible tells us, "All the widows stood by him weeping, showing the tunics and garments which Dorcas had made while she was with them" (v. 39). Dorcas had been a valued and loved member of the church in Joppa and subsequently has become known throughout history for her acts of kindness.

The example of Dorcas reminds us of the emphasis the Bible places on the care of widows and orphans. For instance, James 1:27 states, "Pure and undefiled religion before God and the Father is this: to visit orphans and widows in their trouble, and to keep oneself unspotted from the world." In the Book of Acts, we find a great deal of time being devoted to caring for widows. It was one of the primary responsibilities of the deacons (see Acts 6). However, this is a ministry that is often neglected in our churches today. With the number of widows, single mothers and fatherless children increasing, this work is needed now more than ever.

The ministry of Dorcas also shows us that the gift of compassion is just as important—if not more important—as the more miraculous gifts, such as the gift of healing. Jesus made this very clear in Matthew 25, where He spoke of the Judgment. He stated that only those who had fed the hungry, clothed the naked, housed the stranger, cared for the sick and visited the prisoner would share in His glorious kingdom (see vv. 31-46). Why? "Assuredly, I say to you, inasmuch as you did it to one of the least of these My brethren, you did it to Me" (v. 40). At no other time in history has this need been so great. Jesus, in the form of millions of hungry and distressed people, is still waiting for the hands of mercy to be extended by sincere Christians. Are you responding to these cries for help?

When Dorcas died, many people deeply mourned her. Will the same be true of us when we die? While we should not desire greatness or the praise of men and women, we should still seek to live in such a way that we will be missed by some when we are gone because of our service to them. Even more importantly, our service should be the kind that will cause people to look away from us and to our wonderful Lord, who makes such service possible. If we do not have this quality and quantity of good works, then we need to ask God to help us live as Dorcas did. While we might never have numerous societies named after us as she did, we will have the joy of doing God's will, of making life richer for others and of hearing the Lord say to us, "Well done, good and faithful servant" when we see Him in glory.

God's Wonderful Work

The Lord chose to work through Peter and Dorcas in different ways, but the result was the same. When the people of Lydda, Sharon and Joppa saw the power of the Lord displayed in the healing of Aeneas and the raising of Dorcas, many believed in Jesus (see Acts 9:35,42). The doors were wide open for witness in those cities. No doubt as these new converts gave their enthusiastic testimonies and witness, even more people were attracted to the Lord. In a real sense these breakthroughs had even greater significance than the fact that Peter had healed a paralytic and had raised someone from the dead. God's power to change lives is the biggest miracle of all.

Today, in various parts of the world, we are seeing harvests very similar to those of Lydda, Sharon and Joppa. Among certain tribes and peoples, an overwhelming majority have turned to the Lord and received Him as their Saviour. I have had the privilege of seeing some of these results firsthand. In the mountain communities of western South America, entire tribes of Indians are responding to the message of salvation. Consequently, these communities glow with God's beauty and love.

We need to ask ourselves the questions, *Am I living and testifying in such a way that people in my church, my city and my state are coming to know the Lord? Am I allowing the Holy Spirit to work through me, as He did through Peter and Dorcas?* When we faithfully do the work the Holy Spirit has called us to do—no matter how insignificant it may seem—then we will see the power of God in action. While methods and gifts may change, the harvest will remain the same, for the Lord will cause our efforts to bear much fruit. Some of us may be called to be a Dorcas—unobtrusively performing deeds of kindness. Others may be called to be a Peter—powerfully preaching the message of salvation. Some are called to sow the seed; others are called to water it. But ultimately, the increase will come from God alone (see I Cor. 3:6-8).

Chapter 7

Open Doors
(Acts 10:1-33)

Luke, the writer of Acts, relates the story of Cornelius and Peter in detail because it marks one of the most significant events in the history of the Church. The lesson Peter learned on the housetop took a long time for him to absorb. However, even though he didn't understand everything that God was trying to teach him, we do credit him with putting into practice what he did know. It would be a long time before Peter and his colleagues would really comprehend the truth that the Gospel was for everyone—Jew and Gentile alike—without partiality. Even today, almost 2000 years later, believers still do not really understand the depth of God's love for lost people of every race and class.

Preparing the Man

In Acts 10 the scene shifts from Joppa to Caesarea, located 60 miles northwest of Jerusalem. This city was the headquarters for the Roman government in Palestine. Here we meet the man who would become the Lord's instrument in opening the doors of the Gospel to the Gentiles—the

79

Roman centurion, Cornelius. He was the captain of 100 men for the Roman army and, as such, wielded a great deal of influence. Cornelius was also what the Jews termed a "God-fearer." He was a devout man who reverenced and worshiped the Lord, practicing many of the Jewish rituals. However, he had not been circumcised and thus could not be considered a proselyte Jew. Cornelius's devotion to God was so great that his entire household followed his example. He demonstrated his piety by his generous giving and his constant prayers to God (see vv. 1,2).

Cornelius was obviously a good, moral man. He displayed all the characteristics of a Christian. Yet this passage makes it clear that he was not a Christian. For all his genuine piety, Cornelius still needed God's salvation through faith in the Lord Jesus Christ. Herein lies an important lesson for us today. William Arnot, 19th-century Scottish preacher and scholar, summed it up well when he wrote: "If any man could be just with God, apart from faith in Christ crucified, surely this is the man. A better specimen of humanity you can nowhere find; yet the word of God treats him as a sinner, and forthwith proceeds to tell him what he must do to be saved. There is no escape from the force of this case. It effectually shuts out all hope in the merit of a man. In presence of this word every mouth must be stopped, and all the world become guilty before God. If this man could not appear before the judgment-seat until his sins were blotted out in the blood of the Lamb, how shall we appear with our own sins or our own goodness marked to our account?" (*Studies in Acts,* p. 220).

Even though his good works and piety could not save Cornelius, nevertheless the Lord honored the centurion's desire to know Him by giving him the opportunity to hear the Gospel. The angel of the Lord told Cornelius, "Your prayers and your alms have come up for a memorial before God" (v. 4). God never ignores the person who sincerely seeks Him. Such a person will receive fuller and greater light. John 1:9 declares that Jesus, the true Light, "gives light to every man who comes into the world." God places within every person an inherent knowledge of Him. Ecclesiastes 3:11 tells us, "He has put eternity in their hearts" (see also Rom. 1:19,20). But even more than this, the person who seeks to know God has His promise: "And you will seek Me and find Me, when you search for Me with all your heart" (Jer. 29:13). Jesus reiterated this promise when He declared, "Ask, and it will be given to you; seek, and you will find; knock, and it will be opened to you. For everyone who asks receives, and he who seeks finds, and to him who knocks it will be opened" (Matt. 7:7,8).

These promises encourage us as we tell others about the Lord Jesus. We can be assured that the Lord will lead us to those who are searching for Him. Of course, some skeptics—and even sincere Christians—will no doubt ask, "But what about the people who are never given an opportunity to hear the Gospel? Will they be lost even though they have not heard?" Only the Lord knows the answer to

81

that question. We must simply trust His wisdom and judgment. Thus, our answer is this: "Shall not the Judge of all the earth do right?" (Gen. 18:25). The Lord has promised to respond to all who seek Him, and we can trust Him to keep that promise. Therefore, we should not become enmeshed in hard questions we don't really understand but should instead spend our energies on what we do understand, namely that the Lord Jesus calls us to share the Gospel with these people.

I have seen many modern-day examples of how the Lord leads those who seek Him. One Ecuadorean woman's story parallels the account of Cornelius in many ways. This woman lived in a rural area of Ecuador about three hours from the capitol city of Quito. She became fascinated with the Christian programs she heard on HCJB in Quito. When she became ill, she told her family that she wanted to be treated at the HCJB hospital. She came to Quito, received medical care and also heard more of the Gospel. While there, she learned that the medical department of HCJB sponsored rural medical caravans. She pleaded with them to come to her area. Finally, the HCJB caravan was able to include her area in their schedule. Meanwhile, she had prepared well for their coming. She had told her family and friends all about the Gospel message she had been hearing. After the first day of the medical clinic, the missionaries held an evangelistic service in the village. That night Mrs. Estrada and 16 other family members and friends received Christ as their Saviour. This ministry has grown until there are now several flourishing churches in that area. Once again God had kept His promise to reveal Himself to those who seek Him.

As Cornelius sought the Lord in prayer, he received the answer he had been waiting for. An angel appeared to him in a vision and instructed him concerning what he should do: "Now send men to Joppa, and send for Simon whose surname is Peter. He is lodging with Simon, a tanner, whose house is by the sea. He will tell you what you must do" (Acts 10:5,6). When the angel had departed, Cornelius responded immediately. He called for two of his household servants and a trusted soldier. He explained to them what had happened and quickly sent them to Joppa. Cornelius's example of obedience and trust is an inspiration and challenge to us.

Preparing the Messenger

Long before Cornelius's representatives set out for Joppa, the Lord had begun to prepare His messenger for their arrival. The vision Peter received in Acts 10 was merely the culmination of God's efforts to show the apostle that the Gospel was for everyone. It had begun back on the Day of Pentecost when, under the guidance of the Holy Spirit, Peter had heard himself saying, "I will pour out of My Spirit on all flesh" (2:17). He had also told the people, "Whoever calls on the name of the Lord shall be saved" (v. 21). No doubt Peter pondered the meaning of these words many times in the coming months.

Then Peter, along with John, was given further

confirmation of this when he saw the Lord's work in Samaria through the witness of Philip (see ch. 8). This showed Peter that God was visiting the Samaritans as well as the Jews. As Peter continued this ministry in Judea and Samaria, the words of Jesus must have come back to him again and again: "You shall be witnesses to Me in Jerusalem, and in all Judea and Samaria, and to the end of the earth" (1:8). Then the Lord broke down Peter's prejudices even further by leading him to stay in the house of Simon, the tanner, who was considered by the Jews to be unclean because of his work with dead animals.

Patiently the Lord was enlarging Peter's vision, and slowly—but surely—the apostle was beginning to understand. Like Peter, we often learn the lessons of faith very slowly. Thankfully, our Saviour is a patient and kind teacher; He will lead us one step at a time to the place He has prepared for us.

As the messengers of Cornelius approached the city on the day after they started their journey, Peter had gone up to the roof of the house to pray at about noon. He had only been there a short time when he became hungry and called down for something to eat. But before the servants could finish the preparations, the Lord caused Peter to fall into a trance (see 10:9,10).

In his vision Peter saw the heavens open and an object that looked like a giant sheet descend toward him. Inside the sheet he discovered a huge mixture of animals and birds. Then Peter heard an unbelievable command from the Lord: "Rise, Peter; kill and eat" (v. 13). This law-keeping Jew couldn't believe his ears! The Lord was asking him to defy the prohibitions of Leviticus 11 concerning certain foods. So he naturally protested, "Not so, Lord! For I have never eaten anything common or unclean" (v. 14). Although Peter's response was natural, it was also illogical. Since the Lord had given these rules regarding food in the first place, He had the right to change them if He chose to. The Lord pressed this truth home to Peter, telling him, "What God has cleansed you must not call common" (v. 15).

Once more we see the patience of our great God. For Peter's sake, the Lord repeated this lesson three times (v. 16). Soon Peter would understand that these words referred to much more than merely the ceremonial laws regarding food. Although it would take some time for Peter to accept fully what the Lord was telling him, he did finally realize that the old order was passing away and was finding its completion in the new. Even though he didn't completely understand the Lord's new order, he accepted and carried out God's instructions in simple obedience to His will. The Lord calls us to do the same.

Proclaiming the Message

From this point the story develops quickly. Even while Peter was still pondering the meaning of his vision, the messengers of Cornelius arrived at the gate and asked for Peter. The Holy Spirit gave Peter another nudge, telling him, "Behold, three men are seeking you. Arise therefore, go down and go with them, doubting nothing; for I have sent them" (Acts 10:19,20).

Peter obeyed the Holy Spirit and went to meet the men. After a brief conversation, he invited them into the house. This simple act of hospitality represented an important step forward for Peter. Jews did not ordinarily lodge with Gentiles. But that night an interesting group of people occupied the same house: Simon the tanner, Peter the apostle, two of Cornelius's household servants and a soldier of his command. It was a small illustration of the unity that the Gospel brings.

The next day Peter went with Cornelius's emissaries to Caesarea. He took six fellow believers from Joppa with him (see v. 23; 11:12). When Peter was later asked to explain his actions before the Jewish Christians in Jerusalem (see ch. 11), these witnesses were able to corroborate his story. Even though Peter still didn't fully understand his vision or the Lord's words, we give him credit for obeying to the best of his ability.

When Peter and the other brethren arrived in Caesarea, Cornelius was waiting for them. He had already called together his close relatives and friends. When Peter entered the house, Cornelius fell down at his feet and worshiped. But Peter quickly put a stop to it. He lifted Cornelius up and said, "Stand up; I myself am also a man" (10:26). Throughout the Book of Acts, we see the apostles repeatedly rejecting all undue adulation. They adamantly refused any form of worship. Like John the Baptist, their motto was "He must increase, but

I must decrease" (John 3:30). They knew that worship and reverence belonged solely to their glorious Lord. Even though we know this to be true, we are often tempted to seek praise and honor for ourselves. We must avoid this trap, giving God all the glory for His work in our lives.

As Peter looked around the room at the Gentiles who were waiting with rapt attention to hear the Lord's message, he finally realized the full significance of his vision. He told the group, "God has shown me that I should not call any man common or unclean" (Acts 10:28). I'm sure that Peter could hardly believe what he was saying. But he left no doubt about this truth. He affirmed that God loves all people equally. He does not show partiality. The Gospel is for everyone without exception. People of every race, class and condition can come before the Lord confidently in repentance and faith with the certainty that they will receive His free gift of salvation. Peter had come to realize this great promise, and he desired Cornelius and his friends to know it also. He then added, "Therefore I came without objection as soon as I was sent for. I ask, then, for what reason have you sent for me?" (v. 29).

Now it was Cornelius's turn to explain. He told Peter about his vision and what the Lord had instructed him to do. Then he made a great declaration: "Now therefore, we are all present before God, to hear all the things commanded you by God" (v. 33). Earlier in this beautiful story we learned that Cornelius was a devout man. Now his actions proved it. He lived for God and listened to

87

God. He and his household had open hearts. And open hearts always lead to open doors of blessing.

At this point, I must ask myself, *Do I have that kind of attitude before God? Am I always interested in hearing what God has to say to me? Is my heart like good soil where the Word of God can be planted and bear much fruit?* Cornelius demonstrated tremendous faith in calling his family and friends together to hear someone he didn't know give a strange message. We possess a much greater knowledge of the Gospel. Therefore, our faith in the Word of God should go far beyond that of Cornelius.

Many times, as we have gone into new areas to preach the Gospel, we have found people like Cornelius. They have shown a great hunger for truth and a strong desire to hear God's message. On one occasion, I went to a city in southern Ecuador to participate in an evangelistic campaign. When I arrived in that city, the local missionary told me that a man from a nearby town had come to speak with me. He had heard me on the radio broadcasts of HCJB. When I met him, he overwhelmed me with his lively interest in spiritual matters. He listened intently to everything I told him. Before our conversation had ended, this man had received Christ as his Saviour. I felt as Peter must have felt in the home of Cornelius. Incidentally, shortly after his conversion, my new brother in Christ resigned his government job to prepare for full-time Christian service. He has continued faithfully in the work of God.

Like Cornelius, many people are still waiting

anxiously to hear the priceless message of salvation. The Lord has commissioned us to take that message to those who have not heard—regardless of their race, religion or social class. Like Peter, we need to put aside our prejudices and step out in obedience to the Lord's command, remembering His words to us: "This gospel of the kingdom will be preached in all the world as a witness to all the nations, and then the end will come" (Matt. 24:14).

Chapter 8

Through the Open Doors
(Acts 10:34-48)

In the Book of Acts, we find three "Pentecost" experiences. The first and the largest occurred in Jerusalem on the Day of Pentecost. Peter preached a powerful message to the Jews gathered there, and about 3000 people received Christ as Saviour (see Acts 2:1-41). The second "Pentecost" took place in Samaria through the ministry of Philip. The response of the Samaritans to the Gospel was so overwhelming that the church in Jerusalem sent Peter and John to help. In this case, the Lord withheld the gift of the Holy Spirit from these believers until Peter and John came, prayed for them and laid their hands on them (see 8:5-17). This second great outpouring of the Holy Spirit was needed to show the Jewish Christians that the Gospel was meant for the Samaritans as well.

Now we see a third "Pentecost" taking place among the Gentiles. As Peter shared the Gospel with Cornelius and his household, "the Holy Spirit fell upon all those who heard the word" (10:44). Once again the Lord was confirming in a dramatic way that the Gospel and its benefits are available to everyone everywhere without exception.

Coming to the Open Doors

In his message to Cornelius and his household, Peter underlined four great truths: (1) God shows no partiality; His salvation is offered to everyone equally. (2) Jesus lived, died and rose again in order to make this salvation available to us. (3) We can know that this is true, for we have the testimony of those who witnessed it. (4) Through Jesus, all who believe in Him will receive forgiveness of their sins. This is the heart of the Gospel message. The Lord has opened wide the doors of salvation. As people come to these open doors, we need to share these same four truths with them. When we do, then we—like Peter—may have the privilege of seeing them walk through the open doors. Let's examine each of these important points more closely.

First, we see that Peter had finally learned the lesson the Lord had been teaching him: "In truth I perceive that God shows no partiality. But in every nation whoever fears Him and works righteousness is accepted by Him" (Acts 10:34,35). Peter now realized that the Lord's criterion of acceptance is not based on appearance but on attitude. He looks at a person's heart, responding to even the slightest response or desire to know Him. Without exception, the Lord "desires all men to be saved and to come to the knowledge of the truth" (I Tim. 2:4).

At this point, Peter was able to leave his isolationist Jewish background and culture behind and to

91

see people as God viewed them. However, he still struggled with his old prejudices from time to time. Later, when some of the Jewish believers questioned his views, Peter began to have some doubts and to vacillate. He stopped associating with the Gentile Christians whenever the Jewish Christians were around, and Paul had to reprimand him for not standing his ground (see Gal. 2:11,12).

I fear that many believers are like Peter. They sincerely believe that every person is made in the divine image of God and therefore has infinite worth in His eyes. They realize that God shows no favoritism but loves all people equally—and expects us to do the same. However, in practice, these believers still show partiality in their attitude toward, and treatment of, certain people. Racial prejudice or preference should have no place in the Christian's thinking. We need to heed the words of James, who wrote: "My brethren, do not hold the faith of our Lord Jesus Christ, the Lord of glory, with partiality" (James 2:1). We should read James 2:1-13 often and put its teachings into practice in our lives and in our churches.

Once Peter had assured his listeners that God offers His salvation to everyone, regardless of their race or spiritual condition, he then proceeded to share with them the heart of the Gospel message—the life and work of Jesus Christ. He told them how Jesus had been sent by God and had been anointed with the Holy Spirit and with power. The apostle then described the Lord's earthly ministry: "Who went about doing good and healing all who were oppressed by the devil, for God was with Him" (Acts 10:39). I've always appreciated this passage because it describes perfectly what Jesus did. In both His words and His actions, He was continually doing good to others. No other life can compare with His. He was the perfect man, as well as the Son of God.

But even more important than the life of Jesus was His death and resurrection. Because Christ conquered sin and death, we can overcome them as well through faith in Him. Peter drove this point home as he told these Gentiles how Jesus had willingly given His life, allowing the Jews to crucify Him. Even greater still was the fact that "God raised [Him] up on the third day, and showed Him openly" (v. 40). Jesus Christ is more than a dead prophet— He is a living Saviour. This great truth is what separates the Gospel of Jesus Christ from all man-made religions.

"Furthermore," Peter told the group, "you can believe that Jesus died and rose again because I and many others have seen it" (see v. 39). Peter and the other disciples could give personal testimony concerning the life, death and resurrection of Jesus Christ. After Jesus rose from the dead, they ate and drank with Him. And Jesus Himself had commanded them to tell others about what they had seen and heard (see vv. 41,42).

Throughout the New Testament, we see this same pattern of witness. The believers simply told others about what they had seen and experienced. And at the center of every message was the death and resurrection of Christ, for this is the Gospel. We can see this emphasis in the words of the Apostle Paul: "For I delivered to you first of all that which I also received: that Christ died for our sins according to the Scriptures, and that He was buried, and that He rose again the third day according to the Scriptures" (I Cor. 15:3,4). The fact that Peter and many others had witnessed these things added validity to their testimony.

While we were not eyewitnesses to the death and resurrection of Christ, this does not mean that the Gospel is any less valid today. We have the testimony of the prophets, who foretold the work of Christ, and the witness of those who saw the fulfillment of these prophecies. When we share the Gospel with others, we need to point them to these proofs in the Scriptures, as well as to tell them what the Lord has done in our own lives. As these people come face to face with Christ in the Word and realize what He has done for them, they should be compelled to say, "My Lord and my God!" (John 20:28).

Once Peter had opened the door of salvation to Cornelius and his household and pointed the way to the One who offers this salvation, he expressed the greatest truth of all: "Through His name, whoever believes in Him will receive remission of sins" (Acts 10:43). Anyone can come in simple faith to the Saviour and receive forgiveness of his sins and eternal salvation. But while God has placed in us the desire to know Him and has provided the means by which we can know Him, we must still come to the Light and freely accept it. There is no other way to be saved (see John 14:6). Renowned theologian G. Campbell Morgan expressed this well when he wrote: "Oh, the glad and glorious surprise of those ultimate days when we find that there will be those who walked in the light they had, and wrought righteousness, and were acceptable to Him; not because of their morality, but by the infinite merit of the Cross, and by the fact that they yielded themselves to the light they possessed" (*The Acts of the Apostles,* p. 281).

Walking Through the Open Doors

While Peter was still speaking to Cornelius and his household, the Holy Spirit filled the listeners, and they began to speak in tongues and to magnify God. The Jewish Christians who had accompanied Peter were astonished. They were amazed not only at what they were seeing and hearing but at the fact that Gentiles could receive the Holy Spirit as they had (see Acts 10:44-46).

Why did this special outpouring of the Holy Spirit occur? First, even though the passage doesn't specifically say so, we can conclude that Cornelius and the others believed the Gospel and gave a unanimous response in their hearts to the preaching of Peter. Acts 5:32 states that God gives the Holy Spirit to those who obey Him. Since Cornelius and his friends had received the Holy Spirit, we can conclude that they had obeyed God. Likewise, on the Day of Pentecost, Peter assured the people that if they repented, they would receive the gift of the

Holy Spirit (2:38). Consequently, these Gentiles must have repented.

Second, I believe this special, dramatic outpouring was needed to prove to the Jewish Christians who were present that the Gentiles could be saved. If these new believers had not demonstrated the outward manifestations of the Spirit's power, it is doubtful that the Jewish Christians would have accepted their salvation as genuine. Thus, a third "Pentecost" was necessary to convince them of God's work. This becomes evident in Peter's response to what had happened. He exclaimed, "Can anyone forbid water, that these should not be baptized who have received the Holy Spirit just as we have?" (10:47). In other words, Peter was saying, "How can we not welcome these believers into the fellowship of the Church, seeing how they have received the same salvation and Spirit that we have?" This direct act of God forced them to accept the Gentiles as fellow brothers in Christ.

Peter's response brings up another interesting point. This passage records that the new believers were baptized. Since these men and women had already been filled with the Spirit and evidenced their faith in several ways, Peter and the others could have concluded that the ceremony of baptism wasn't needed. But Peter commanded that they be baptized. This shows us the importance of baptism.

When we observe the Christian world, we discover two extremes. Some groups place too much emphasis and importance on baptism. They make it a requirement for salvation. Other sectors fail to give baptism the importance it should have and forget that Jesus commanded believers to be baptized. That was a part of the Great Commission. If He commanded it, we had better obey. Peter sought to be obedient to his Master and therefore urged baptism for the new believers.

Meaning of the Open Doors

Following this tremendous conversion experience, Cornelius and the other new believers asked Peter to stay with them a few days (see Acts 10:48). They were undoubtedly pondering the meaning of their new life and were needing someone to explain the Scriptures more fully to them. They still had much to learn. Likewise, devout as Cornelius was, no doubt he saw some areas of his life that needed to be changed. Furthermore, they had a big task before them in witnessing to their wider circle of friends. So Peter stayed to instruct them in the Scriptures that would serve them in their life and witness for Christ.

This practice of discipleship is strongly stressed in the New Testament. When Jesus gave the Great Commission, He told us to go and make disciples, "teaching them to observe all things that I have commanded you" (Matt. 28:20). Whenever possible, we should do what we can to help those we win to Christ to mature in their Christian lives.

The second reason why Peter remained with Cornelius and his friends was because of what it would mean in his own ministry. God had taught him not to consider any person common or unclean.

Soon he would be called to share this truth with other Jewish Christians. Therefore, it was important that he display this truth in his actions, as well as in his words. And what better way to do this than to remain as the guest of Cornelius for a few days? Peter had never done anything like that before. He must have experienced a great deal of culture shock. I imagine sleep didn't come easily for him that first night. He may have asked himself, *Am I doing the right thing? What will my friends say? Will the other apostles agree with me?* But yet he realized that he was merely following what the Lord had taught him, so he was obviously doing what was right. This knowledge would give him strength to speak boldly when called upon to defend his actions in Jerusalem. God's way is always best—even when it means that we must go against the majority.

The conversion of Cornelius and his household opened the doors of the Gospel to everyone everywhere. Through the centuries, God's message has remained the same. He loves all people equally. In every nation those who fear Him and desire to know Him will be accepted by Him. He has opened the doors of salvation wide. All that remains is for us to enter through the open doors into His presence and then to lead others to do the same. May God help us and inspire us to take His Gospel to the nations still waiting to hear.

Chapter 9

Preparing for Larger Outreach
(Acts 11:1-18)

Thus far in our study of this portion of the Book of Acts, we have seen several tremendous events take place—events that would forever shape the destiny of the Church. First, Philip preached the Gospel to the Samaritans. Then he led the Ethiopian eunuch to the Lord, thus opening the way for non-Jews to hear the Gospel. Third, the greatest persecutor of the Church, Saul of Tarsus, became a convert and began to preach powerfully about Christ. Finally, Cornelius and his household trusted the Lord Jesus as Saviour. At the same time Peter learned the great lesson that the Gospel is for every person, no matter what his race, religion, social class or spiritual condition.

No doubt the early Christians were thanking God for these advances. Nevertheless, they were discovering that forward movement often brings major changes in relationships. These believers found themselves being carried along in the dramatic transition from Old Testament ceremony to New Testament realities. And like us, they probably felt threatened by these changes. To some, it may have seemed as if the past and the present were colliding rather than merging. I often wonder how you and I would have handled this situation. The writer Luke considered this experience so important that he devoted a great deal of space to the story of Cornelius's conversion and the contention that arose from it.

Confusion and Contention

When the other apostles and believers in Jerusalem heard what had taken place in Caesarea, many were confused and alarmed. The more conservative, law-keeping Jewish Christians couldn't understand why Peter and the others were suddenly transgressing cherished traditions and eating unclean food with unclean people. They considered such conduct to be heretical and scandalous. While they didn't object to the Word of God being preached to the Gentiles or to their accepting Christ, they believed that these new converts should live by the old Jewish laws and regulations.

So these confused believers criticized Peter and contended with him over the issue. In this passage we note that the Greek word translated "contended" (Acts 11:2) is the same word the writer of Acts used to describe God's dealings with Peter and Cornelius. We read in Acts 10:20: "Arise therefore, go down and go with them, doubting [contending] nothing; for I have sent them." In Acts 11:12, Peter reiterated these instructions, stating, "Then the Spirit told me to go with them, doubting [contending] nothing." Because these believers had not participated with Peter in the experience, they didn't understand what God was trying to teach them. Consequently, they were doubting Peter and his actions, disputing with him because he had broken Jewish regulations.

We can understand their confusion. Throughout their lives they had carefully obeyed God's laws of diet and conduct. They had kept themselves pure by not eating unclean foods and by remaining separate from unclean people. Now they were seeing a complete reversal of these practices. To make matters worse, Peter—one of the chief apostles—was spearheading this revolution. However, they had forgotten one very important fact: Peter was following the example of his Saviour, who had also smashed some sacred cows. Jesus had frequently acted in ways that appeared scandalous to those bound by man-made traditions or to those who didn't understand that He was the fulfillment of these prophecies and ceremonies. For example:

—His teachings about the Sabbath emphasized the spirit of the observance instead of legal rule making.

—His treatment of despised sinners demonstrated an attitude of love instead of condemnation.

—He ate with publicans and sinners. He accepted the Samaritans, who were scorned by the Jews.

Down through the years, others have listened to God's voice instead of man's opinions. They have blazed new trails in the face of fierce opposition. For example, Reformers such as Luther, Calvin and

101

Zwingli spoke out against the doctrines and practices of the established church. Many of their enemies condemned them as heretics. However, the Reformers were right. Because of their efforts in returning to the teachings of the Bible, today we also stand for the authority of the Word of God and the doctrine of justification by faith.

The life of William Carey is another case in point. He called the people of his day to involvement in world evangelism. He went to India as a missionary despite determined opposition from many of his colleagues in the ministry. Because of his dedicated service, he is known today as "the father of modern missions."

Similarly, Clarence Jones and Reuben Larson had the conviction that God was calling them to use the new instrument of radio for Christ on the mission field. Their critics called them crazy. However, they listened to God instead of their critics and founded mission radio station HCJB in Quito, Ecuador. As a result of the efforts of these men and many others since then, radio now reaches around the world to areas where missionaries cannot go.

On the other hand, change can sometimes be detrimental, and we need to resist it. The present-day change in family values is one good example. Today vast numbers of unbelievers are attacking the biblical concept of the family. Chastity and fidelity in marriage is no longer stressed in our society. Divorce, adultery and child abuse are rampant. Likewise, many people today support the so-called alternate life-styles. However, the Bible strongly condemns homosexuality and other such "life-styles," and so should we. The justification and promotion of abortion is another example. A simple reading of Psalm 139 should convince us of how wrong abortion is. We should speak out against these practices, using the clear teachings of the Word of God as our support.

As we consider these controversies, may our prayer be "Lord, make me an open-minded conservative. May I be a person who stands firmly on the fundamental truths of the Bible. May I never base my faith on my own pet interpretations of the Bible or on traditions not taught in God's Word. May I be someone who can distinguish between principles that do not change and methods that can change."

Conduct and Clarification

Because the believers in Jerusalem were confusing Jewish traditions with the Bible's teachings, they did not understand what the Lord was trying to teach them in the conversion of Cornelius. Instead of supporting Peter's actions, they criticized and condemned him for associating with Gentiles.

Notice how Peter responded to his critics. Instead of becoming haughty, angry or defensive, he quietly listened to their questions and accusations and then patiently tried to clarify what had occurred. As he explained, he did not argue heatedly or intimidate the believers by reminding them of his special authority as an apostle. Instead, he simply presented the facts and let them decide for themselves

103

if his actions had been proper or not. Peter's conduct under fire is an example to us of how we should handle criticism. It also teaches us an important lesson about leadership. Peter may have been reflecting back on this incident when he later wrote: "Shepherd the flock of God which is among you, serving as overseers, not by constraint but willingly, not for dishonest gain but eagerly; nor as being lords over those entrusted to you, but being examples to the flock" (I Pet. 5:2,3).

It's also important to note how Peter developed his defense. He began with his personal testimony. He told them about his dream, concluding with the Lord's important words to him: "What God has cleansed you must not call common" (Acts 11:9). He then related how the angel had instructed him to go with the messengers of Cornelius. Peter stressed to the believers that his work with the Gentiles had not been an arbitrary decision on his part. Instead, he had merely responded to the leading of the Lord.

Some people today would argue that personal testimony should not have a place in our witness. Of course, we must be careful how we use it, for it is subjective and open to challenge. In addition, some people have misused it, teaching false doctrine under the guise of a special "calling" from God. We should test any "calling" by the Word of God, for the Lord does not call us to do anything that contradicts His teachings in the Bible. However, if the Lord has indeed dealt with us in a special way, we should not hesitate to share that experience with others.

In defending his actions, Peter not only appealed to his calling from God, but he supported his testimony with well-documented facts. He told the believers how he had followed God's guidance and preached the message to Cornelius and his family, adding, "And as I began to speak, the Holy Spirit fell upon them, as upon us at the beginning" (v. 15). There was no mistaking the fact that the hearers had believed and had been filled with the Holy Spirit. Peter and the six others who had accompanied him were witnesses to the miraculous manifestations of the Spirit's power in them. Cornelius and his household had been forgiven of their sins and had received the Holy Spirit—all without having submitted to the Jewish rituals.

Finally, Peter showed how the teachings of the Scriptures supported what had taken place. He told the group, "Then I remembered the word of the Lord, how He said, 'John indeed baptized with water, but you shall be baptized with the Holy Spirit'" (v. 16). Peter found his strongest argument in the Word of God. When we confront decisions and choices, we must also look to the Bible for our answers. Likewise, when we are asked to defend our beliefs and actions, we should always appeal to the highest authority—God's Word.

In Peter's defense to the believers in Jerusalem, we discover the criteria we should use in judging any new idea or in evaluating any change to determine if it is from God. We must ask ourselves three questions:

1. Has this idea come as a result of prayerful

consideration and sensitivity to the guidance of God?

2. Is it supported by objective information and facts?

3. Is this idea or change supported by Scripture? Does it contradict any clear teaching in God's Word?

If the idea or change passes these three tests, then we can usually be certain that we are following God's will in the matter.

Confession and Cooperation

After Peter had calmly and decisively answered the criticisms of the crowd, the Bible tells us, "When they heard these things they became silent" (Acts 11:18). The believers stopped disputing and contending with Peter and became silent to give opportunity for thought. They didn't say, "My mind is made up. Don't confuse me with the facts." Instead, they carefully weighed what they had heard and then allowed the message to sink in.

Many Christians today would do well to follow their example. We have a tendency to talk more than we listen. We spend our time defending our opinions rather than seeking to know the truth by searching God's Word in fellowship with other sincere believers. We're often like the man I heard about who was contending vigorously in a congregational meeting. Most of the members wished to obtain a new chandelier for the church building. He was opposed to the idea, arguing, "First, it's too expensive. Second, I can't spell it. Third, what we need is better lighting." We laugh at this gentleman's ignorance, but sometimes we act just as foolishly. May God help us to follow the good example of these believers, who listened carefully to Peter's testimony, facts and appeal to Scripture and then became silent as they humbly reflected on what they had heard.

As the believers prayerfully reflected on Peter's words, it finally became obvious to them that the Lord was at work in this situation. As a result, "they glorified God" (v. 18). These Jewish believers willingly confessed that they had been wrong in condemning Peter and the Gentiles before they knew all the facts. They no doubt apologized to Peter and commended his actions, for they changed their opinions regarding salvation for the Gentiles.

At this point we need to ask ourselves, *Am I as willing to admit when I am wrong? When I unduly criticize someone or something and then receive a clarification of the facts, do I apologize to that person and change my viewpoints on the matter?* I trust that we do, for this is the way in which a Christian should respond.

Not only did the believers willingly admit that they had been wrong in judging the Gentiles, but they demonstrated their change of heart by their attitude of cooperation and support. They finally realized that the Gospel was for everyone—Jew and Gentile—without exceptions or restrictions. They declared, "Then God has also granted to the Gentiles repentance to life" (v. 18). In making this declaration, they

107

were also stating their willingness to take the Gospel to the Gentiles.

In just a few short hours, we see a group of believers moving from contention and dispute to acceptance and cooperation. The lesson is obvious. Problems and contentions will arise in almost every congregation, because believers often do not view certain matters in the same way. These contentions become even more evident during times of change and progress. When difficulties do arise, we need to work with our leaders in seeking God's guidance, in gathering the facts and in reaching conclusions that are firmly grounded in the Word of God. When we follow this approach, our congregations will prosper. However, when believers refuse to listen to the opinions of others or to change their own erroneous views after they've heard the facts, then their congregations will suffer division and heartache.

How then do we handle contentions in the church? By remembering that while God and His Word never change, the methods He uses to accomplish His purposes can, and do, change. Thus, we must ask the Lord for wisdom to know the difference between His *timeless principles* and the *temporary methods* we can use to proclaim His message to others.

Chapter 10

A Movement With Impact
(Acts 11:19-30)

The Book of Acts covers just 33 years. In that short time, fervent witnesses preached the Gospel throughout the known world. If that kind of dynamic had continued, the world would have been reached for Christ many times over. Almost all historians of that period, sacred and secular, call attention to the ardor of the early believers. "O God, to us may grace be giv'n / To follow in their train!"

In Acts 11 we witness one of the greatest events in church history. For the first time the early Christians deliberately shared the Gospel with the Gentiles. Of course, Philip had gone to the Samaritans previously, but they were half Jewish. And Peter had preached to Cornelius and his household, but he had done it by divine invitation and compulsion. But in this passage we see humble believers spontaneously going to the Gentiles.

Let's look at the setting for this great drama—the city of Antioch in Syria. Antioch was the third largest city of that day—behind Rome and Alexandria—with a population of more than 500,000. It lay 300 miles north of Jerusalem and about 16 miles east of the Mediterranean Sea. The city stood on the main travel-and-trade route to Mesopotamia (present-day Iraq). Because of its location, Antioch became the center of government and culture in that part of the world. People from many different nations lived there, including a sizable population of Jews. In many ways Antioch was an attractive and cosmopolitan city. However, it had also earned a reputation for luxurious pleasure and gross immorality. The citizens had a fanatical devotion to chariot racing.

Antioch was also famous for its worship of Daphne, a pagan religion that centered around prostitution. The temple to this goddess was located five miles outside of Antioch near a grove of laurel bushes. Legend said that Daphne was a mortal woman with whom the Greek god Apollo fell in love. He pursued her, and she was eventually turned into a laurel bush for her protection. In the religious ritual, the worshipers and the temple prostitutes would reenact the love scene in the laurel groves. Into this perverse atmosphere came the persecuted believers with the powerful message of the Gospel. Before long, many of the Daphne worshipers left that immoral religion and became followers of the Son of God.

The People God Used

It's amazing that such a wicked city could become the center of Christian outreach and growth. This story becomes even more remarkable when we consider the people God used to accomplish this

110

feat. The Lord did not call great preachers, such as the Apostle Peter, for the task but instead used simple laymen who had suffered for their faith. Acts 11:19-21 tells us that the believers who had been scattered because of the persecution spearheaded by Saul traveled northward to Antioch and the surrounding cities, preaching the Gospel as they went. At first they witnessed to the Jews only, but then some men from Cyprus and Cyrene began sharing the Gospel with others. Soon many Gentiles were coming to the Lord. Because their faith had cost them so much, it had infinite worth to these believers. They were anxious to share it with others.

The founding of the Antioch church is a vivid example of how suffering often leads to blessing. Therefore, when suffering comes into our lives, instead of becoming bitter or despondent, we should allow the Lord to accomplish His work through the trial. And when we are not experiencing hardships, we should watch carefully that we do not backslide in our spiritual lives. When we enjoy good health, have material abundance and are blessed with good friends and family, we can easily forget our need for the Lord.

We see these two principles illustrated in the Church of Smyrna and the Church of Laodicea in the Book of Revelation. The believers in Smyrna suffered overwhelming poverty and persecution. Nevertheless, Jesus said about them, "You are rich" (2:9). This church was blessed through its suffering and became alive and vibrant because of it. On the other hand, the Church of Laodicea

111

enjoyed great material prosperity. Yet Jesus rebuked the believers, telling them, "You are wretched, miserable, poor, blind, and naked" (3:17). Why? Because the church was spiritually bankrupt.

When we look for blessings to come from our suffering, then we can have joy in the midst of our trials. The early believers possessed overflowing joy even while facing severe persecution. When the authorities in Jerusalem were threatening these believers, they did not hide in fear but instead gathered to praise the Lord (see Acts 4:1-31). Later we read that the Thessalonian Christians had the same spirit. They received "the word in much affliction, with joy of the Holy Spirit" (I Thess. 1:6). We can serve the Lord and witness for Him most effectively when we do His work in the joy of the Lord. Like the believers of Antioch, joyful Christians are a great blessing to others.

In Acts 11 we see how God used ordinary believers—believers who had suffered greatly yet still served joyfully—to begin one of the most important churches in history. As we read this passage, we especially notice that the names of these Christians are not given. Even though they were just as important as Philip, Peter and Paul, they have received no acclamation for their accomplishments. Instead, they served quietly and effectively, not seeking the praise of people. And while they may be unknown to us, they are known by God and will receive their rewards from Him.

What the church needs most today is servants who will work and not care who gets the credit for it.

Right now I think of numerous Christian brothers and sisters in churches and missions. They are almost anonymous, but they have done great things, started great awakenings and sparked marvelous revivals. Though not known to people, they are known by God. I have some friends whom God has used greatly as fishers of men. They go about their witness quietly, for they are not seeking the praise of men. I've also been in touch with very generous donors who take great care that their giving does not become known by others. They desire God to receive the honor. Such Christians belong to the same class as the founders of the Antioch church. Although they did a great work, we don't even know specifically who they were.

The Attitude God Honored

When the church in Jerusalem heard about the tremendous outreach taking place in Antioch, the leaders sent Barnabas on an information-gathering mission. They could not have commissioned a better man. Barnabas had the biggest heart in the church. He had stood by Saul when others were doubting his salvation (Acts 9:27). He had given proof of his Christian love through his overflowing generosity (4:36,37). The only quarrel we know Barnabas had came as a result of his determination to give another chance to a man who had failed (15:36-39). He was the perfect man to help the fledgling church in Antioch.

In Antioch, Barnabas once again demonstrated why he was known as the "son of encouragement."

113

When he saw the grace of God at work in the church of Antioch, he rejoiced with them and for them (11:23). Other representatives might have exhibited a different attitude. They might have said, "These believers in Antioch don't have an apostolic commission to do what they are doing" or "These Gentiles must submit to Jewish law before we can allow them into the Church." They even could have declared, "So what if the church here is growing by leaps and bounds? It won't last." But Barnabas showed no signs of legalism or jealousy. He sincerely rejoiced because God was working gloriously in the Antioch church.

Some of you may be thinking, *Why are you placing so much emphasis on this attitude? Isn't it natural? Shouldn't we rejoice in the grace of God at work?* Yes, we should. But most of us would have to confess that we easily fall into the trap of rejoicing in our own blessings and achievements but not in those of others. We must remember that, in Christian life and service, a victory on one front is a victory for the whole army. We will truly promote the work of the Lord if we genuinely support every area where we see Him moving. This is true even when what others do doesn't fit neatly into the methods or ideas we are comfortable with. Like Barnabas, let's rejoice whenever and wherever we see the grace of God at work.

Barnabas displayed this kind of spirit because he was filled with the Spirit. The Bible describes him as "a good man, full of the Holy Spirit and of faith" (11:24). In this short sentence we discover the formula for becoming a good person. Goodness is part of the fruit of the Spirit (Gal. 5:22). Therefore, it is produced when we are filled with the Holy Spirit, which occurs as a result of faith. Thus, goodness comes only by unwavering trust in Jesus Christ and not by anything we do. And this kind of goodness enables us to show love to others in ways that no person of himself could do.

Not only did Barnabas rejoice with the believers in Antioch over what the Lord was doing there, but he "encouraged them all that with purpose of heart they should continue with the Lord" (Acts 11:23). The church in Antioch had been founded and blessed by God because of the faith of the believers there. Barnabas told them that as long as they continued to live by faith, the Lord would continue to bless them. We find this same encouragement in Colossians 2:6: "As you have therefore received Christ Jesus the Lord, so walk in Him." So often in the Christian life we have spurts of activity followed by periods of apathy. We are constantly on a spiritual roller coaster. This is usually the result of depending on our own strength and abilities. Only total dependence on the Lord will make us constant, persevering and faithful in our Christian life.

During Barnabas's ministry in Antioch, the Bible tells us, "A great many people were added to the Lord" (Acts 11:24). Barnabas had become a key leader in the Antioch church. He was greatly respected and had a good ministry among the people. But notice what he did: "Then Barnabas departed for Tarsus to seek Saul. And when he had

115

found him, he brought him to Antioch" (vv. 25,26). Barnabas was experiencing a growing conviction that Saul could have an important ministry in Antioch. He went in search of Saul, all the time realizing that Saul would probably take over his role as leader in the church. But this didn't matter to Barnabas. He only cared about the welfare of the church and the glory of the Lord Jesus. Such selflessness will always advance the cause of Christ.

Imagine what marvelous things we would see happening in our churches today if every believer displayed the selflessness of Barnabas! Of all the attitudes that Christians are called to have, this one is no doubt the hardest to learn. A listener once asked an orchestra conductor what was the hardest instrument to play. Unhesitatingly the conductor replied, "Second fiddle." May we all follow the example of Barnabas in our willingness to rejoice in the victories of others, in our encouragement of fellow believers and in our selflessness to share leadership for the welfare of the whole church.

The Principle God Blessed

Barnabas went to Tarsus in search of Saul and brought him back to Antioch to help in the ministry there. They then spent an entire year teaching and training the church in Antioch (Acts 11:26). Saul and Barnabas knew the importance of teaching in the Christian life. They wanted the believers of Antioch to know God's truth and to know it well. This same principle is true today. One of the primary responsibilities of churches is to provide solid

116

Bible training to help believers grow to maturity in Christ.

Christian growth and maturity does not happen overnight. It is a process that continues throughout our Christian life. God is not in a hurry. He spends a great deal of time preparing His soldiers for service in His mighty army. We see this throughout Scripture. The Lord spent almost 80 years preparing Moses to deliver the Children of Israel from bondage in Egypt—40 years as the adopted son of Pharaoh's daughter in Egypt and 40 more years in the wilderness of Midian. Jesus did not begin His public ministry until He was 30 years of age. He in turn spent three years intensively training His disciples to carry on the work.

We see this principle at work in the life of Saul as well. Before Saul was ready to teach the believers in Antioch, God spent almost ten years preparing him for service. After Saul escaped from Damascus (9:30), he returned to his hometown of Tarsus, where he remained until Barnabas asked him to go to Antioch ten years later. No doubt the waiting had been hard for Saul, but he had needed that time in personal study and communion with the Lord in order to prepare him for the difficult ministry that lay ahead. Now he was ready for the task, and the task was waiting for him.

Leadership and lasting ministry take preparation. Before we can effectively serve, we must spend time alone with God. Too often we desire to be spiritual astronauts without undergoing the training. We

117

want to become Olympic champions without having to practice. Instead of worrying why we are not being used or noticed, we should spend our time and energy in preparing ourselves for what God has in store for us. Then, once we have passed the Lord's intensive training course, we will be ready to enter the ministry He is calling us to.

Saul and Barnabas properly prepared themselves for their teaching ministry, and as a result, they had a wonderful year of fellowship and instruction with the church in Antioch. As I've indicated before, the early church quickly welcomed new believers. The only credentials they needed were faith in Jesus Christ with the resulting presence of the Holy Spirit. But afterwards the leaders made sure that they received thorough grounding in the Word of God. The church needed this preparation for the demanding role it would continue to play in world evangelism.

I've seen this principle of teaching at work in a church-planting ministry in Lima, Peru. Some leaders there felt led by God to establish churches on several of the principal avenues of that city. They began by holding several evangelistic meetings in a large house they had purchased on one of those streets. Then they held a Bible conference for the new converts. They repeated this process of evangelism and Bible teaching a number of times until the congregation of believers was large enough to warrant the construction of a church building. Through the use of this system, three large churches have been planted in the city of Lima. All three of these congregations continue to make the teaching ministry an important part of church life.

The secret of success in the Christian life lies in the principle of Bible teaching. We need this preparation in order to weather the storms of life. Spiritual immaturity only leads to sin and sorrow. However, the Lord blesses those who study and obey His Word. When we are well grounded in the Word, we will experience security in our Christian lives and will see our service blessed.

The Testimony That Resulted

In Acts 11:26 we see the results of the teaching that the Antioch believers had received. In this passage we learn that "the disciples were first called Christians in Antioch." We don't know if the name was given to them in mockery or respect. But it does show that these believers were living in such a way that the people around them realized that they belonged to Christ and that He was the head of the Antioch church. The Greek word translated "Christians" literally means "Christ-folk." I wonder what name people would give to us today if they observed us and chose a label that would best describe us? Would it be the name "Christian"?

Some years ago a missionary asked Mahatma Gandhi, "What suggestion do you have for us to make Christianity more indigenous to India?" Without hesitation Gandhi replied, "You must look more like Jesus Christ." An excellent answer from a man who was not a professing Christian.

Not only could the image of Christ be seen in the

witness of the Antioch believers but in their compassion as well. When they learned of the famine in Judea, they immediately collected a relief offering. They considered this offering so important that they sent Barnabas and Saul to deliver it personally to the saints in Judea (see vv. 27-30). What a beautiful ending to this part of the Antioch story! The believers in Antioch show us a pattern for Christian living. As their knowledge of Christ increased, so did their love and compassion for others. Slowly they were being molded into the image of Christ so that others couldn't help but notice it.

The highest achievement in the Christian life is that of attaining Christlikeness. This will have more impact on the world than anything else. The Lord Jesus will mold us into His image through the Holy Spirit when we commit ourselves totally to Him. We do not need to have a great deal of money or talent to do important work for the Lord—only a thirst for God and a great love for our Saviour. As we allow ourselves to be led by the Holy Spirit in all areas of our lives, then Christ will do His work in and through us.

Chapter 11

A Strange and Beautiful Story
(Acts 12:1-19)

We often say that truth is stranger than fiction. Robert Ripley capitalized on this fact with his *Believe It or Not* series. In it he would show and describe some amazing—but true—events, places, people, animals and facts. The Bible also contains some amazing—but true—passages, including this one in Acts 12. These verses relate the strange, yet beautiful, story of the execution of James and the imprisonment and miraculous rescue of Peter. When we see how God was at work in these situations, we can only give praise and glory to Him.

A Story of Death and Deliverance

As Acts 12 opens, we see a fresh outbreak of persecution beginning, led by King Herod Agrippa I. His observance of the Jewish laws and rituals had made him popular among the people. In order to increase his popularity and influence among the Jews, he seized the Apostle James, brother of John, and had him beheaded in A.D. 44. When he saw how much this pleased the Jews, he proceeded to have Peter arrested, intending to have him killed

121

as well. However, it was the week of the Passover, and it was illegal to hold a trial and execution during that time. So Herod had to imprison Peter until after the Feast of Unleavened Bread was completed (see vv. 1-4). But before the king could carry out his evil plans, the Lord would intervene and miraculously deliver Peter from prison.

When most people read this passage, they frequently ask, "Doesn't it seem strange that God would allow James's life to end so abruptly while sparing Peter's life?" Some have erroneously concluded that the Lord did not intervene for James because he was not as important to the work as Peter was. However, the Bible gives no support for this view. James must have had a significant ministry, or Herod would not have chosen him for execution.

This incident is not an isolated case either. From Bible times to the present, we can ask the same questions concerning others. For instance, why did Stephen become the first martyr, while Paul escaped death on numerous occasions? Why did Corrie ten Boom survive her years in a concentration camp, while her sister died there? Why did Bible translator Chet Bitterman lose his life at the hands of terrorists in Colombia, South America, while four missionaries captured by another terrorist band in the same country were set free? Why were five young men killed in the jungles of Ecuador as they sought to take the Gospel to the unreached Auca tribe, while many missionaries have gone to this tribe and others in Ecuador since then and have had their lives spared? Why did Stan Dale and Phil Masters suffer martyrdom in Irian Jaya, while author and fellow missionary, Don Richardson, was able to reach another dangerous tribe in that area without losing his life?

I believe that part of the answer to these questions can be found in the account of the great heroes of the faith in Hebrews 11. This chapter begins by recounting the tremendous achievements, rescues and triumphs by faith of many well-known people in the Old Testament. But the chapter concludes with a list of faith heroes who "had trials of mockings and scourgings, yes, and of chains and imprisonment. They were stoned, they were sawn in two, were tempted, were slain with the sword" (vv. 36,37). In this passage we see that the group who was delivered was no greater than the group who died. Some were simply saved *from* great problems by faith, while others were saved *in* the problems by faith.

While only the Lord knows the reasons why He has chosen to take some people and spare others, we do have a wonderful principle that provides the foundation for an answer. We know from the teachings of Scripture that God is love (I John 4:8-11). He is also wise and powerful. This means that He desires our good, knows what is for our good and can accomplish our good. So we know that in everything He works for His glory and for the highest good of His people. Therefore, in the case of Peter and James, we can conclude that Peter's ministry was not yet finished while James's had been completed. For that reason, under God's loving care, James's life was taken and Peter's was spared. No matter what God calls us to do, we can trust Him, for He knows what is best and will work for good in every situation.

A Story of Peace and Power

Peter spent the next week in prison, knowing all the time that the same fate awaited him that had befallen James. In order to insure that he would not escape, Herod had assigned four quaternions of soldiers to guard him. Each quaternion was made up of a squad of four soldiers. These four squads would rotate at regular intervals during the day and night. They knew better than to allow the prisoner to escape, for to do so would cost them their lives.

No doubt Herod took these extra precautions because he remembered what had happened when the Jewish authorities had tried to imprison Peter and the other apostles. The officials had "laid their hands on the apostles and put them in the common prison" (Acts 5:18). But an angel had come to the prison at night and set the apostles free, telling them, "Go, stand in the temple and speak to the people all the words of this life" (v. 20). The next morning, when the Jewish leaders summoned the guards to bring the prisoners before the Council, they discovered to their amazement that the prison doors were shut, the guards were standing at attention but the prison cell was empty. Adding insult to injury, a messenger arrived at that moment and told them, "Look, the men whom you put in prison are

124

standing in the temple and teaching the people!" (v. 25). Herod did not want to be embarrassed as these officials had been.

On the night before his scheduled execution, we find Peter lying in that dark prison, chained between two soldiers with two more soldiers guarding the door—*sound asleep*. It seems incredible that Peter could sleep at a time like that. First, the miserable conditions of the prison and the discomfort of the chains would seem like enough to keep most people awake. And as he considered what was about to take place, his natural reaction would have been to feel anxious and depressed.

However, strangely enough, we do not find Peter worrying. Even though he knew that he might also become a martyr for the faith, he was not anxious about it. Why? Because he was experiencing the peace of God. He knew the Lord was in control of the situation, and therefore, Herod would not succeed in killing him unless God allowed him to for some reason. Because Peter had faith in God and had the peace of God, he could feel completely secure—even in Herod's prison.

Every Christian can experience the same peace in the storm, the same assurance in danger and the same joy in difficulty, for we have the same Saviour that Peter had. We also have the same promise: "The peace of God, which surpasses all understanding, will guard your hearts and minds through Christ Jesus" (Phil. 4:7). Therefore, we need not be anxious but should instead place our burdens at the feet of Jesus in prayer (see v. 6).

Nowhere have I seen this peace more visibly displayed than in the lives of the Christians in China. On a recent visit to China, I visited two couples who had suffered harsh persecution and imprisonment under Chairman Mao's government, especially during the days of the Red Guard. These special people demonstrated great peace and joy because their faith and hope were fixed in the living, all-powerful Lord.

Peter displayed calmness and assurance in the face of death because he was filled with the peace of God and trusted the Lord to do what was best. And, in this case, the Lord chose once again to deliver Peter. The angel of the Lord appeared next to Peter and struck him on the side, rousing him from his sound sleep. When Peter opened his eyes, he saw a bright light around him and heard a voice telling him, "Arise quickly!" (Acts 12:7). As he struggled to his feet, he felt the heavy chains drop from his wrists. We don't know all the details, but it is evident that the soldiers were unaware of what was taking place. Peter even had time to gird himself, tie on his sandals and put on his garment. Then, still in a daze, he followed the angel past the first gate and then the second one—both heavily guarded—and out of the prison. When they reached the iron gate leading to the city, it opened automatically. As they walked past the first street, the angel suddenly disappeared. Peter realized that he hadn't been dreaming after all. He was really free!

God's power has not diminished in the least through the years. He can still rescue and free His people today. As a college student, I remember reading the book entitled *A Thousand Miles of Miracle in China* by A. E. Glover. It told of God's remarkable deliverances during the chaotic days of the Boxer Rebellion. In my many years of missionary service, I have witnessed what the Lord can do for His people. I remember one example of God's miraculous power in particular. Missionary radio station HCJB had just completed the construction of their large new antenna and transmitter site near a small rural town not far from their headquarters in Quito, Ecuador. Several fanatics in the town were opposed to having this "evangelical" broadcast installation nearby. So they made plans to destroy the transmitters and antennas. But when they attempted to execute their plans, an unseen power kept them from doing so. Try as they might, they could not destroy these facilities. Some years later, several members of that group told us about what they had attempted. We believe, of course, that the angel of the Lord thwarted this destruction.

Like Peter, we need not be afraid or anxious when we are facing danger and difficulties. Rather, we should confidently place our lives and our resources in the Lord's powerful hands, allowing Him to fill us with His marvelous peace. The same great God who delivered Peter can meet our needs today.

A Story of Supplication and Surprise

As we read this beautiful story of the deliverance of Peter, we especially notice the role that prayer played in his rescue. We see here what can happen when God's people band together in fervent prayer. The Lord answered the prayers of these believers in a special way.

When Peter was arrested and thrown into prison, the Christians in Jerusalem immediately met together to pray. In this passage, we note two important aspects of their prayers. First, we see the intensity of their praying: "But constant prayer was offered to God for him by the church" (Acts 12:5). Charles B. Williams in his translation has rendered this passage: "Earnest prayer to God for him was persistently made by the church." The believers were praying continually for Peter during the days he was imprisoned. The Greek word translated "constant" or "earnest" is the root word from which we get the one used to describe Christ as He prayed in the Garden of Gethsemane (see Luke 22:44). Other passages of Scripture where the key word "constant" or "earnestly" is used are I Peter 1:22: "Love one another *fervently* with a pure heart," Luke 22:44: "And being in agony, He prayed more *earnestly*" and Acts 26:7: "Twelve tribes *earnestly* serving God night and day" (italics added). The different usages of this word in the New Testament reveal to us the intensity and fervency of these believers as they prayed.

Second, we note the number of believers who participated in this prayer meeting on behalf of Peter. Acts 12:12 tells us that a sizable group had gathered together in the home of Mary, the mother of John Mark. In other words, their praying had both *quality* and *quantity*. Many believers were praying fervently. And the Lord has committed Himself to answering that kind of prayer. When people observe our prayer meetings in our local churches, can they see that we have both quality and quantity? Do our missionaries receive that kind of prayer support? I trust so. When we begin to pray this way, then we will begin to see the Lord answer our prayers in miraculous ways.

The account of what happened after Peter left prison makes us smile. Peter went directly to the house where the believers were praying. He knocked at the door of the gate, and a girl named Rhoda came to answer. When she heard Peter's voice, she became so excited and glad that she ran to tell the others but left Peter standing outside the gate. When she told the people at the prayer meeting, they said, "You're crazy." When she insisted, they said, "It's his angel."

But Peter kept knocking. Choleric Peter became impatient. I can just hear him saying, "It's easier to get out of Herod's prison than to get into a Christian prayer meeting!" Finally, it appears that most of the folks went to the door to see for themselves. Sure enough, they saw Peter and were astonished. But they shouldn't have been. Weren't they praying for his release? Why should they be surprised when God answered? Often we are like them, aren't we?

However, let's not be too hard on these believers. They had prayed earnestly, and God had answered. I take comfort in finding this story in the Bible. Even though these believers didn't have perfect faith,

129

God still answered. We may look foolish, as the folks in Mary's house did, but God still loves to answer the prayers of His children. Those early believers were not super people; they just believed in a super God. Often we need to say, "Lord, I believe; help my unbelief!" (Mark 9:24).

Today we still have the powerful channel of prayer available to us. We live in a sinful, needy world. Often we face problems that are beyond our ability to handle. But we can be at peace because we know that our Lord is in control. He will take care of us. Therefore, "be anxious for nothing, but in everything by prayer and supplication, with thanksgiving, let your requests be made known to God" (Phil. 4:6).

Chapter 12

The Blasphemer Blasted and the Believers Blessed
(Acts 12:20-25)

Charles Simeon, the great Cambridge preacher, made some significant observations about pride. He stated that pride is dangerous for two reasons: First, it *denies God's goodness.* We must always remember that everything we have comes from God. Second, it *invades God's prerogative.* (*Expository Outlines on the Whole Bible*, p. 407). As Creator and Sustainer of the universe, God alone deserves all the glory. It should not be given to any other person (see Isa. 42:8).

In Acts 14:8-18, when Paul had healed a crippled man at Lystra, the people thought that he and Barnabas were gods. They showered the men with garlands and intended to sacrifice oxen in their honor. How did Paul and Barnabas respond? They tore their clothes and said, "Why are you doing these things? We also are men with the same nature as you" (v. 15). They then urged the multitude to trust and worship the living God. Instead of accepting the praise and worship of the people, Paul and

Barnabas pointed them to the only One who deserves our worship.

When we are being praised and honored for our accomplishments, we are often tempted to take full credit for them. However, we should never yield to that temptation. Instead, we should give glory to God for the way He has used us. In the story before us, we find the people praising King Herod and calling him a god. Herod made the mistake of accepting the plaudits of the people. As a result, he was judged by God. He learned the hard way that the Lord will not share His glory with another.

Herod's Pride

Proverbs 16:18 tells us, "Pride goes before destruction, and a haughty spirit before a fall." We find no better illustration of this warning than the life of King Herod. His vanity and pride led to deadly results.

Who was Herod, and what kind of a man was he? In answering these questions, we first need to clarify which Herod is being referred to in this passage in Acts 12. In the Gospels and the Book of Acts, we learn a great deal about the family known as Herod, who ruled Palestine during this period. The story begins with Herod the Great, who reigned over all of Palestine from about 41 B.C. to 1 B.C. He had ten wives and a number of children, many of whom he had executed. He was an evil and vicious ruler. He was responsible for rebuilding the temple in Jerusalem that was later destroyed in A.D. 70 by the Romans. He was also the Herod who was in power when Christ was born (see Matt. 2:1-18). He was the one who spoke to the Magi from the East and who massacred the children in Bethlehem.

After the death of Herod the Great, the regions of Palestine were divided among his sons. The Romans granted power over Judea, Samaria and Idumea to Herod Archelaus (see Matt. 2:22). He was so wicked and bloodthirsty that he was deposed and banished after ten years in power. His region was then placed under the authority of a Roman procurator. Herod Antipas, the second husband of Herodias, was the tetrarch of Galilee and Perea. He consented to the death of John the Baptist and was the one to whom Pilate sent Jesus for trial. Herod Philip II, the most loved and kindest of the Herods, was the ruler of Iturea and Trachonitis (see Luke 3:1). He was the founder of Caesarea Philippi.

Following the deaths of Antipas and Philip, Herod Agrippa I, the grandson of Herod the Great, came into power. He had been raised and educated in Rome and was a close friend of Claudius Caesar. Because of this relationship, he was the only Herod to be made a king. He was also given complete control of Palestine once again. In an effort to win the favor and support of the Jews, he practiced all of the Jewish customs and rituals. Because of his desire to please the Jews, he also began to persecute the Christians in Jerusalem. He arrested the Apostle James and had him beheaded. He then seized Peter, intending to execute him also, but God thwarted his plans.

These incidents shed a great deal of light on

133

Herod Agrippa's character. The people of Tyre and Sidon soon realized that they could receive favors from Herod by appealing to his vanity. In Acts 12:20 we learn that Herod was angry with these residents. Herod's disfavor had grave consequences for them, because they depended on the food that he controlled. So they plotted to regain his friendship. They succeeded in winning the support of Blastus, one of Herod's trusted officials. They may have bribed Blastus or appealed to his pride in other ways. Through Blastus, they made their desire for peace known to Herod. During a festival held in Caesarea to honor the Roman emperor, a large group from Tyre and Sidon assembled to hear Herod deliver a speech.

Herod dressed for the occasion in his best royal apparel. Josephus, the Jewish historian, tells us that Herod was wearing a magnificent silver robe that glistened in the sun. He must have been a striking figure as he spoke to this group. During his speech, the crowd repeatedly shouted, "The voice of a god and not of a man" (v. 22). Their praise of Herod probably contained more flattery than sincerity. They knew what to say to please Herod and win back his favor. And Herod absorbed these acclamations like a dry sponge. He reveled in being called a god. He was not able to bask in this praise for long though, because he soon experienced the wrath and judgment of God.

We quickly recognize how foolish Herod was. We find it easy to condemn him. However, before we do so, we should recognize that we all have a tendency to be proud. Consequently, we need to pray constantly that we will have the spirit of Jesus, who was "gentle and lowly in heart" (Matt. 11:29). We can overcome our attitude of pride by remembering that "God resists the proud, but gives grace to the humble" (James 4:6).

God's Punishment

God's judgment of Herod was immediate and final. In Acts 12:23 we read: "Immediately an angel of the Lord struck him, because he did not give glory to God. And he was eaten by worms and died." According to the best sources of that time, Herod collapsed with severe abdominal pain. He spent five days in agony before he finally died. Josephus recorded the words Herod spoke as he realized what was happening to him: "I, a god in your eyes, am now bidden to lay down my life, for fate brings immediate refutation of the lying words lately addressed to me. I, who was called immortal by you, am now under sentence of death. But I must accept my lot as God wills it" (*Antiquities* XIX, 347-350, as quoted in *The Expositor's Bible Commentary*, Vol. 9, p. 413).

From this incident we learn a solemn lesson about the futility and sin of pride and about the judgment and justice of God. Although God's justice often does not come as dramatically or swiftly as it did in the case of Herod, it *will* come just as certainly. Throughout the Bible, the Spirit of God warns us concerning the inescapable result of sin. Galatians 6:7 tells us, "Do not be deceived, God is not mocked; for whatever a man sows, that he will also reap." In Romans 12:19 we read God's emphatic promise: "Vengeance is Mine, I will repay." Hebrews 10:31 reminds us, "It is a fearful thing to fall into the hands of the living God."

In light of the certainty of God's judgment, what should our attitude be? First, we must take these warnings to heart ourselves. We must be certain we have made our peace with God through the perfect sacrifice of our Lord and Saviour, Jesus Christ, and are living according to His will. Second, we must be diligent to warn men and women about the coming judgment. All around us people are marching to judgment and a Christless eternity. In portraying this terrible reality, Amy Carmichael pictured these people as flowing over a terrible precipice to certain doom, while Christians were seated nearby casually making daisy chains. God forgive us if we have that attitude! May we call people everywhere to repentance and faith in Jesus Christ so that they will not only escape God's judgment but will enjoy His blessings for eternity.

The Church's Prosperity

Once again we see the Church prospering in the face of persecution. Acts 12:24 tells us, "But the word of God grew and multiplied." Just when it appeared that Herod was gaining the upper hand, the Lord intervened on behalf of the Church and protected the believers. When Saul was persecuting the believers, the Lord's power changed him

136

into a new person. In this case, God chose to work in a different way—by eliminating the enemy. But the result was the same. God blessed His Word, and the Church continued to grow.

Both in the Book of Acts and in churches today, we find God working in much the same way. Often when the Church appears to be headed for tragedy and destruction, it is instead standing on the threshold of its greatest triumph. The Lord frequently does His most powerful work when believers are the weakest and their enemies are the strongest. God delivered Peter at one of the lowest points of his life—as a prisoner awaiting execution. Likewise, He punished Herod at the highest point of his self-sufficiency. Frequently, God allows us to go *through* the fire in order to set us *on* fire. Churches and individual believers often do their best work for God in the worst situations. As we look at the Christians who are suffering persecution and tragedy in many areas of the world, we can see this principle at work. These believers exhibit a beautiful dedication to the Lord. Many of the strongest and most mature churches exist in countries where Christianity faces intense opposition.

Today we face many problems in our countries, our Christian organizations, our families and our own lives. Instead of becoming dismayed over the difficulties, we should say, "Lord, use these trials to help us do a greater, more powerful work in Your name. Make us everything You want us to be."

Recently one of our sons and his wife passed through a difficult trial. They decided to employ in

137

their business two people who had been in trouble with the law. They wanted to help rehabilitate these two individuals. However, one of the employees sued them for discrimination, and the other stole from their customers. In telling us about the problem, our son and daughter-in-law said, "It's been hard to take. We've suffered anguish and loss. But in the difficulty we have trusted God more and have learned good spiritual lessons."

When we walk with the Lord, we can turn trials into triumphs, problems into petitions, grief into growth, sorrow into service and frustration into fervor. Like the psalmist, we need to say, "It is good for me that I have been afflicted, that I may learn Your statutes. . . . I know, O Lord, that Your judgments are right, and that in faithfulness You have afflicted me" (Ps. 119:71,75).

God knows how to turn burdens into blessings. And in the process, we grow spiritually and glorify Him even more. This is just one of the ways in which God equips His people and His Church. The Church in Acts went through terrible trials but came out of them equipped for larger service. Throughout the Book of Acts, we find the early believers marching like a mighty army, using their greatest weapon—the sword of the Spirit—to defeat their enemies. They displayed such power that their enemies could only declare in amazement, "[They] have turned the world upside down" (Acts 17:6). In reality, they were bringing it right side up! May we allow the Lord to equip us as He did those early believers so that we, too, might turn our world upside down as we share His great message with people everywhere.

O Wind of God, come bend us, break us,
'Til humbly we confess our need;
Then in Your tenderness remake us,
Revive, restore—for this we plead.

O Heart of Christ, once broken for us,
In You we find our strength and rest;
Our broken contrite hearts now solace,
And let Your waiting Church be blest.

Bibliography

Arnot, William. *Studies in Acts.* Grand Rapids: Kregel Publications, 1978.

Barclay, William. *The Acts of the Apostles,* rev. ed.; (*The Daily Study Bible Series.*) Philadelphia: The Westminster Press, 1976.

Bruce, F. F. *Commentary on the Book of the Acts.* (*The New International Commentary on the New Testament.*) Grand Rapids: Wm. B. Eerdmans Publishing Co., 1954.

Harrison, Everett F. *ACTS: The Expanding Church.* Chicago: Moody Press, 1975.

LaSor, William Sanford. *Church Alive.* Glendale, California: Regal Books, 1972.

Longenecker, Richard N. *John—Acts.* Vol. 9 of *The Expositor's Bible Commentary.* General editor, Frank E. Gaebelein. 12 vols. Grand Rapids: Zondervan Publishing House, 1981.

Lumby, J. Rawson, ed. *The Acts of the Apostles.* (*The Cambridge Bible for Schools and Colleges.*) Cambridge: Cambridge University Press, 1921.

Macaulay, J. C. *Expository Commentary on Acts.* Chicago: Moody Press, 1979.

Morgan, G. Campbell. *The Acts of the Apostles.* Old Tappan, NJ: Fleming H. Revell Company, 1924.

Scroggie, W. Graham. *The Acts of the Apostles.* (*Study Hour Commentaries.*) Grand Rapids: Zondervan Publishing House, 1976.

Simeon, Charles. *John XIII—Acts.* Vol. 14 of *Expository Outlines on the Whole Bible.* 21 vols. Grand Rapids: Zondervan Publishing House, 1955.

Thomas, David. *Acts of the Apostles.* Grand Rapids: Kregel Publications, 1980.

Walker, Thomas. *Acts of the Apostles.* (*Kregel Expository Commentary Series.*) Grand Rapids: Kregel Publications, 1965.

Back to the Bible is a nonprofit ministry dedicated to Bible teaching, evangelism and edification of Christians worldwide.

If we may assist you in knowing more about Christ and the Christian life, please write to us without obligation:

Back to the Bible
P.O. Box 82808
Lincoln, NE 68501